Poor No More

Poor No More

Sustainable Solutions to Poverty
in the Social Justice Era

James Conner

RESOURCE *Publications* · Eugene, Oregon

POOR NO MORE
Sustainable Solutions to Poverty in the Social Justice Era

Resource Publications
An Imprint of Wipf and Stock Publishers
199 W. 8th Ave., Suite 3
Eugene, OR 97401

www.wipfandstock.com

PAPERBACK ISBN: 978-1-6667-8532-6
HARDCOVER ISBN: 978-1-6667-8533-3
EBOOK ISBN: 978-1-6667-8534-0

VERSION NUMBER 05/14/24

Contents

Essential Element IV: Project and Organization Leadership
Adapting for Completion and Types of Leadership Roles on the Team

Essential Element V: Adopting New Models for Missions
Bless the Old, Pursue the New

Essential Element VI: Global Exposure for New International Leaders
New Vision Exposure and Practices for Western Partners

Essential Element VII: Growing the Project Through Phases

Introduction

Extreme poverty can be alleviated one village at a time.

There is a path to ending endemic, crippling poverty, and it first takes root in a single community. As it grows in effectiveness, this phenomenon begins spilling over and multiplying in regions. By spreading to nearby communities, it inoculates them from toxic, desperate cycles of poverty and lifts each member of the community into their God-given potential and purpose. I have witnessed this firsthand, and I will show you how to achieve these results.

NEW DIRECTIONS

Change the Focus from Poverty Alleviation to Wealth Creation

The new directions for combating global poverty and its resulting environmental degradation require us to look in new directions. The Hebrew word for changing direction is *sur*.[1] It is derived from ancient pictographs made up of two symbols, a thorn and a head, which represent turning in a new direction.[2] The pain of the current path is what causes the change. So, pain causes us to search for new directions. As we seek to avoid what is currently afflicting us, we veer away from the path we were on. Our new direction is creating locally sustainable and expanding "wealth building" opportunities.

---

1. "Lexicon: Strong's H5493," para. 1–2.
2. Benner, *The Ancient Hebrew Lexicon*, 202.

The Current Way Things Are Done

The current practices of global aid agencies, governments, and NGOs all focus on the same failed strategy: transfer payments. They are essentially moving money, services, food, and education as transfers from wealthy nations and regions to poorer ones. The problem is that moving money without growing local economic systems for sustainability and growth does not work. People need jobs and businesses, not handouts.

Unfortunately, whether this comes from a heart of compassion or a social justice conviction, the identical failed pathways are passionately pursued, and the only difference is the rhetoric. These transfer payments bring about momentary relief from certain afflictions, regrettably accompanied by increased foreign dependance and local structural fragility; yet they fail at changing the overarching systems at play.

When the grant cycle ends, ever worse poverty ensues due to the new foreign dependencies created by the foreign aid itself, leaving people more desperate and disillusioned than before—and without hope. This is compounded by increasing levels of self-doubt, believing they must somehow be inferior to others and that this is why things fail over and over. This false belief of inferiority has murderous consequences as people abandon their own knowledge of their community and become supplicants for every foolish plan proffered on their behalf.

There is a better way.

In this book you will discover how these different systems can positively work together to bring about the long-term, locally sustainable results that we all desire. This is transformational work, and we will need to pause on the rhetoric, biases, and existing structural models and urgencies to engage in a different way of thinking, planning, partnership, and behavior. Every group in the system must renew their thinking to break free of the patterns that do not serve us. Donors, communities in transition, local leaders, churches, governments—all are invited to engagement around different ways of thinking and processing to actually realize the achievable results that form our common goal.

HOW IT STARTED

Nearly two decades ago, I attended an Altrusa Club meeting in my hometown of Arcadia, California. This club of civic-minded individuals with a passion to make a difference had invited me to hear presentations by several African students pursuing graduate degrees in the United States. They shared about what they were learning and the work they planned to do in their communities when they got home to combat extreme poverty and all that it entails.

I was inspired. We hit it off immediately and had great conversations over our shared meal. As time progressed, these students became part of the congregation that I served, and we shared more meals and discussed their future plans. I learned a great deal about poverty, approaches that worked, and traditional approaches that did not.

ESSENTIAL ELEMENTS

Poverty can be overcome when we invest in local, globally exposed leaders and strategically invest capital producing resources in a community to harvest the talent that God has placed in each person within that community, so that it will prosper, grow, and bless others.

This book will cover the essential elements to transforming a community. Each piece is necessary to create the desired change, and as such, projects tend to fail because of omitting one or more of them. These essential elements are also interconnected in many ways. So, in some of these areas as you read, what appears to be a rabbit trail is trying to show you the connections that all of these essential elements have and how they rely on each other.

When you implement the practices in this book, you will be able to work with global leaders in the United States to establish businesses that will support the hospitals, schools, clinics, and so forth that you want to establish, in order to transform a community from poverty dependance to fruitful multiplication, economic expansion, and blessing other nearby communities.

By the end of this book, you will gain an understanding of the beauty, intelligence, and knowledge possessed by local leaders and see why aid-based models (e.g., giving food and clothing) and single solutions to poverty fail. As you better comprehend the underlying conditions of poverty and the poverty mindset, you will be awakened to how you can be actively and personally involved in changing the lives of families in a community. You will be inspired to make a difference in the world in a sustainable and repeatable way, transforming how you do missions and partner in the world, seeing a multiplying effect that will impact neighboring communities and transform how families live. These impacted lives will have resources to touch far more communities, since they will not be trapped in the perpetual funding of an ongoing work but will instead be self-supporting and expanding.

I invite you to be challenged to experience Jesus' teaching on the parable of the talents, and how we are blessed with kingdom authority as our service brings a multiplied return on investment in the lives affected with what has been entrusted to us. You will see the Holy Spirit at work, strategically providing resources, healings, changes in the weather, and favor with politicians that could only be provided by God's miraculous intervention that ultimately brings him glory. Families will be restored and reunited as men find work and purpose again, leaving lifestyles of addiction and abuse and returning to their rightful place as heads of household, leaders, and workers.

No one wants to be seen in a poverty state. God doesn't create people to be poor and impoverished. *He does not!* God gives—generously. God invests. That is why every village and community around the globe already has vast, untapped resources of human talent, giftedness, and vision—a treasure trove of divinely bestowed potential awaiting harvest—more valuable than that of all the holding companies, banks, and hedge funds in the world.

THE OBSTACLES

This is the point where many observers will start to speak about corruption and greed, and why many developing nations cannot move forward. Ironically, almost all of the efforts at alleviating poverty travel through these self-same corrupt systems or rely on the tested-and-failed model of exclusive Western control. In doing so, NGOs regularly circumvent the best and brightest in local communities who have the ability and cultural awareness, which both of these other entities lack in their entirety. We have given politicians and NGOs a free hand, but clearly the solutions from "on high" have not achieved the promised results.

Empowerment, Not Aid

In one of my Transformational Development classes, I was asking the leaders what their goal was for community transformation. One leader from India said, "I want to feed 10,000 children a day." Most of the room was pleased with the boldness and size of this vision, and heads nodded in approval.

I looked at him and kindly replied, "I won't help you with that." He looked shocked, and I let a moment of silence linger in the room. Looking him in the eyes, I said, "But I will help you empower the parents of these 10,000 children to feed their own children in their own homes from the jobs and opportunities that we help create. And not only that, to be able to house them appropriately and pay their school fees."

Then my friend smiled.

VISION

As you read these pages, I implore you to consider undertaking the challenging and fruitful work of creating environments where jobs, careers, businesses, and industries are created and run by managers in a given community, by *partnering with the creative entrepreneurial people in that community*, to the glory of God.

This vision stands in stark contrast to the existing paradigm that desperately needs to change. As the West has continually moved large amounts of money to poorer regions around the globe, the overall results have been underwhelming, to say the least. Unfortunately, compassionate, ongoing aid donations and redistributive justice strategies lead to cycles of dependance and scarcity thinking, which is debilitating. Instead of perpetuating the psychology of dependence, we must make a hard pivot to proactivity and empowerment. These villages are not empty; they are overflowing with potential and opportunity. Building self-sufficiency in the local community is the key to prosperity.

BECOMING EDUCATED

Topics: Terrorists, Poverty, Growing Churches, Orphanages

At that first meal with African leaders many years ago, I learned a lot about local circumstances robbing children of their parents. It surprised me that many orphanages were not legitimate, as many exploit children for the gain of the operators, and some even traffic children. Moreover, the local structures meant that many children would be cared for by the larger village structure if something happened to the parents, and removing them from the village community was often destructive to the children. At a later "unplanned meeting" hosted in my home, a group of leaders from India confirmed similar circumstances in their nation.

Community Transformation

These conversations became the impetus for the community-transformation work that the church and I would later become involved in. This work has evolved and expanded over time to see multiple projects on various continents grow and multiply under local leadership with local autonomy. We have seen local funds expand through local businesses being developed, whose profits fund their ministries and stimulate diversification in the local economy, enabling education, healthcare, water wells, and other services to spring up as well as new agricultural practices and expansion.

Synod of the Nile

About the same time, I was working with a local Egyptian pastor, Hisham Kamel, and we were taking trips to Egypt to train local church leaders in youth and children's work. Eventually, the pastors were invited so the work would have broader acceptance and support in the local churches. This led to me doing multiple trainings on funds development and stewardship with the church leaders. Over time, through a series of unplanned meetings, I was training local pastors how to supplement their incomes through real-estate development by finishing out newly built flats and selling them for a profit. Now the majority of pastors supplement their incomes through this side business.

Church Planting

Also concurrent with this, I was approached by an Indonesian pastor, Bob Jokimon, about partnering with him to start an Indonesian congregation on our church campus. This was the second of ten such church plants, the first being a mainland Chinese immigrant church. These ten churches eventually planted more than thirty churches locally and globally, and I had the opportunity to coach these leaders as their influence and responsibilities expanded, in addition to being invited to do so internationally.

Building Church and Home

During this time, I was also raising funds and renovating the large church campus where I was serving (52,000 square feet). Additionally, I was remodeling the forty-year-old home where my family lived. While remodeling the church, we gave 10 percent of the funds raised to building projects around the world. This put us in Egypt and Uganda, working on schools, church planting, and leading to a seminary expansion, the Evangelical Theological Seminary in Cairo. In this season, a retired missionary from Cairo and Lebanon joined the church, furthering my education of the area and ministry responsibilities and opportunities there.

We also saw changes in the local congregation, as more than twenty different language groups became part of the church—from China and Taiwan to Japan, India, African nations, Indonesia, and Egypt, to name a few.

WHAT IS THE MESSAGE? *SAY YES*

These were events, circumstances, and friendships that we said yes to. We had no special expertise or understanding about what was forming or taking place, or of how God was guiding things and what would come from all of this.

The Team

More than a dozen retired missionaries, World Vision staff, retired pastors, and church mission leaders have been part of learning, following, and forming this process. My role has been to ask questions, stay humble, and gather insights across disciplines, people groups, and from all these learned people, all while learning to keep saying yes when I have no idea what will open up next.

I Am a Skeptic

I must confess, I have been skeptical about many of the invitations and unplanned opportunities I have received. I do not say that with pride, as I have been humbled over and over again at how God continuously weaves things together out of seemingly disparate origins and arenas to create a colorful tapestry of blessing. I have had conversations and relationships with international celebrities, cabinet-level government officials and ambassadors, global denominational leaders, global business leaders and people of influence in commerce, as well as hospital directors, physicians, and regional medical directors. These unique meetings and opportunities have opened doors to incredible blessings, partnerships, and insights with expertises far beyond my humble role as a local church pastor, bridging connections and organizations to see the kingdom come on earth as it is in heaven.

Most all of these strategic meetings took place via a last-minute phone call or text as the invitation to deviate from the plan was introduced with one canceling and another inviting. It typically goes something like this: "Hey, can you come over? There is someone I want you to meet." Or while riding in a car in a city thousands of miles from home, one of my friends or hosts will say, "We have a chance to meet with someone today, so I have shifted our other appointments. Is that OK?"

Say yes.

Or the director of the Clinic in Limbe who, during our impromptu meeting where we arrived and knocked on the door unannounced, said to me, "You need to get in the car. I am taking you to Beau, to the director of our hospitals."

"When do you want to go?" I asked.

"Right now," she replied—and off we went.

Say yes. As I rode the hour-and-fifteen-minute ride up the mountain on a winding road, suffering from the symptoms of typhoid (quite uncomfortable), I wondered what God had in store next. When I met the director and told him my mission, this proud man broke down and told me through tears, "You are not here on your own. Do you realize that? I have been praying and traveling all over Europe for four months because God told me he was going to provide hospital equipment. I spent three months in Germany where I did my residency on this mission with no fruit, and then you arrive in my office unannounced with exactly what we need."

Say yes. Whenever interruptions happen and plans change, just say yes! This has led to meetings and conversations with billionaires, interior ministers, and one local influential elder in a farming community who shared some fresh vegetables and a huge plate of chicken in his home. We later shared a meal together with a former Muslim Brotherhood convert who is leading thousands from another religion to the Lord.

"Trust in the LORD with all your heart, and lean not on your own understanding. In all your ways acknowledge Him, and *He will direct your paths*" (Proverbs 3:5–6, NKJV, emphasis mine).

I AM BLESSED

I am blessed to be influenced by Christian grandparents who gathered me after waffles and eggs to pray for missionaries in Papua New Guinea and taught me about missions and God's love from a young age. My grandfather taught me how to take broken things apart and look for the piece that was not working to fix the whole. That gave me an ability to analyze and problem solve. Without these inputs and many more—from friends who died early and motivated me to realize life is short, to my own children and their encouragement in miraculously overcoming life-threatening illnesses and conditions by God's grace—I am blessed beyond all men, a broken vessel, I pray, leaking grace wherever I go. In God's economy nothing is wasted. God recycles and repurposes everything. This includes things not always desired, but in his economy, they are never wasted.

I have witnesses *real changes* in real people's lives and communities with broken systems that have been transformed by repairing the pieces that were essential but missing. These pages will reveal the essential missing pieces and a process for discovering and partnering with the equally essential and unique *local leaders*, with whom we may prayerfully affect productive mutual engagement that brings about *long-term* transformation and *sustainable* growth and expansion.

JOIN IN

As you read these pages, you are being invited on a journey to reconsider how we engage the global poor and join in what God is already doing. This book is an ongoing compilation of a journey of learning while coaching and training global leaders in the United States and in their own countries through seminars, sermons, guest lectures, consulting, and classes. I have taught at the International Theological Seminary in West Covina, California, and other schools internationally. In this book, we will cover a whole host of topics that will help us make significant inroads into complex systems.

God is up to great things. Chase after what he is doing. Do not get distracted or discouraged by the obstacles of entrenched systems or government corruptions that lie in the way. Just smile and dance around them as you join the lover of your soul in this whirlwind of life, serving the people whom God loves so much "that He gave His only begotten Son, that whoever believes in Him should not perish but have everlasting life" (John 3:16, NKJV).

Missions and Purpose

The purpose of missions is to be used as a channel to release in ourselves and the community the purposes for which God made us and to join him in bringing the kingdom on earth as it is in heaven, bringing people to salvation in Jesus Christ, raising them as disciples, and transforming the world through the redemption of all things (including systems and circumstances) for the glory of God.

Build a Team

This kind of engagement requires talented teams who cooperate and work well together. People with business, education, development, construction, and organizational backgrounds are foundational to bringing the expertise required to fulfill the mandate of Matthew 28:18, of going into all the world and making disciples. God has gone before you and is already lining up the people and resources you have yet to identify that you need. They are waiting for you.

Go in God's power and peace. Shalom.

—James Conner
December 2023
Azusa, California, USA

Essential Element I

Vision

Accessing the Community, Building a Vision,
Identifying Missing Pieces, and Where to Begin

1

Here We Go!

Honing the Vision

"... Behold, the dwelling place of God is with man. He will dwell with them, and they will be his people, and God himself will be with them as their God. He will wipe away every tear from their eyes, and death shall be no more, neither shall there be mourning, nor crying, nor pain anymore, for the former things have passed away... Behold, I am making all things new."

—REVELATION 21:3–5

THINGS ARE BROKEN—FIX THEM

Observations

WALKING TO THE MAILBOX early in the morning, I noticed a piece of chrome trim coming off one of the cars on the street. This particular brown Mini belonged to one of my daughter's college-aged friends sleeping on our floor over the weekend. Bending over, I tried to push the chrome trim back in place and then realized my need for a few tools from the garage, which I used to realign the clips that held this piece of trim under the rear window.

Opportunities

I watched as the yellow rope pulled up the green bucket with the yellow handle, like one we used to take to the beach for my children's building escapades. The bucket hit against the dirt sides of the well, causing little pieces of mud and dirt to fall into the water, while little goats walked around pooping and peeing on the grass near the well opening as a light rain fell. I witnessed this walking through new Bona Ko village in Cameroon with my friend Andrew Jr. and his board members. The summer before, the same leaders of this project had led the villagers in building two classrooms for their new school—to serve what would be the first literate generation of this tribe going back a thousand years.

WHAT IS THE PROBLEM?

Poverty

From human trafficking to lack of education, lack of clean water, food insecurity, pollution, lack of health care, illiteracy, exploitation, poor housing conditions, high crime, prostitution, teen pregnancy, abortion, drug addiction, alcoholism, corrupt governments, and the list goes on, they all have roots in *poverty*.

Common Factors

When sociologists study poverty, they look for common factors that are part of poverty and come up with a common list. It is often assumed that these common lists (e.g., lack of health care, clean water, food security, and education), if addressed, will end poverty. This, however, is conflating symptoms with causes. It is a good discipline to identify the common factors in poverty and to realize that if we are neglecting any one area, we will not have a complete solution.

However, there is an assumption here that these common factors are the cause of poverty and not merely symptoms of poverty.

WHAT ARE THE SYMPTOMS AND
WHAT ARE THE CAUSES?

A high school athlete sustained a knee injury playing sports. He was sent to an orthopedist, who referred him to an orthopedic surgeon, as the knee had no cartilage. After surgery and recovery, the knee was reinjured, and another surgery took place. After the third surgery, a second opinion was sought. After much searching, a diagnosis of lupus SLE was made. The young athlete had an auto immune disease where malfunctioning white blood cells had identified a part of his body as an infection or intruder and was producing these white blood cells to kill it off. Unfortunately, these white blood cells were targeting and destroying the cartilage in his knee.

In medicine and in community transformation, the symptoms do need to be addressed, but the *cause* must first be diagnosed to make sure we are moving toward a cure, or the symptoms will reappear. If we treat just the symptoms, we will likely miss the cause and thereby potentially cause more harm.

WHAT IS THE STRATEGY FOR A SOLUTION?

Complex, Comprehensive Solutions for Complex Problems

The goal is to address the systemic needs in a failed or under-functioning system to identify specific transformational parameters that produce on-going change and expansion. When we only address an individual aspect or a specific problem within a system, which is related to the overall challenges, we often wind up creating other unintended repercussions that can exacerbate and deepen the dysfunction. Thus, we will fail to achieve the necessary systemic, transformational, upward change that is desired.

2

Poverty Defined

SYMPTOMS AND CAUSES

Small Dreams

DURING OUR CLASS DISCUSSION in the "Creating a Vision" section, Davis said he and his partners were struggling with the amount of money they had identified for their project. There was much discussion about the amount being too big, but as they laid out their expenses, it seemed necessary. Still, they could not imagine raising this much money to transform a community; there must be some sort of dollar limit on a project that they should not exceed.

"What is your budget for the total project in all of its phases?" I asked.

"Twenty thousand," Davis replied with a worried look, as if he had just stepped on someone's toes accidentally.

"Yes," I agreed, "twenty thousand is the wrong number."

Davis looked relived and saddened all at the same time.

Then I asked, "How many people are in this community?"

"About twelve thousand, in three villages."

"A better number for that," I asserted, "would be closer to two hundred thousand dollars."

Davis' eyes got really big, and he started to shake his head slowly.

God-Sized Vision

Seeing his incredulity, I began to offer an explanation for my higher numbers: "Davis, you may start with twenty thousand; that would be good seed money. But if you are going to grow and expand at all over the next three to five years, you will be expanding greatly in a variety of areas, and your budget will grow as will your results. Plan for that success, and pray for the resources you need, not what you believe you already have.

"If we want God to be involved in our plans, then our vision must be God sized. If everything we want to accomplish can be achieved by resources we already can identify, it is not a God-sized dream and does not require God's participation. When we pray and seek God diligently and join in what God is already doing, the vision will grow and expand to such an extent that it will be clear *only* God could have done this. To God be the glory!

"*Prepare* various budget strategies around different resource levels so that when a donor comes along a particular level, you have a budget strategy to meet the level of the donor."

DEFINITIONS OF POVERTY CONDITION

More Than Lack of Money

Poverty is a financial condition, yet poverty is more than a financial condition. Poverty is a mindset, an entire belief system, a set of assumptions that guide one's life. It is a way of thinking and behaving; it is living on the outside of society and feeling invisible, neglected, and uncared for. Poverty is a belief system about self-worth, an assumption about God's lesser love for the individual. It is a looming fear of failure, that if things do not go well, great catastrophe and harm will come because there is no backup resource available. We are on our own.

Poverty is a form of fatalism about existing conditions. "This is what we have," the voice of poverty says. "We may get a chicken every now and then, but this is what we have. This is our lot, so we should grab what we can when we can, because this is all there is."

Poverty is a set of assumptions about a limited future. "Because we are poor, even if our children get a break in education or an opportunity, we cannot expect that they will do as well as other people—after all, we are poor." Poverty requires a constant conservancy of every small thing to be reused and not discarded because it may be necessary in the future. "Someday, I am going to fix that and make some money."

Therefore, poverty is a spending pattern that fails to save, a depressive force that welcomes mood-altering substances to relive the suffering. It is constant state of worry and self-doubt; it is an assumption of inferiority of self, related to anyone with more resources. This self-deprecating idea and its accompanying behaviors become a natural, expected pattern of conduct in a cycle of humiliating humility. It is injury and desperation, low expectations and small dreams, which appear to be required by the economic state of being poor and "less than" others.

The Poverty Mindset Says:

- I cannot change my condition on my own. I need help from the outside. Without help I will always be stuck here.
- If I am not careful, I will be right back where I was before.
- Wealth and riches are for others.
- Calamity follows resources and will consume them; therefore, "eat, drink, and be merry," for tomorrow the resources will die.
- If it requires money, I cannot do it.
- If an idea of creating wealth is presented, this is for other people, not for us. We have tried these things, and they do not work here.
- It is too late for me to start. I have missed my chance.
- Even if I tried, I would probably fail again. This time the disappointment would be too much. Please leave me be, before I lose all hope.

Exploited Victim

The poor are also regularly targeted with false promises of future benefits—to buy certain products to resell, or to give up their land under false pretenses and inflated promises that never materialize—under the belief that this must be how others got rich. When exploited by "get rich quick" schemes or unfulfilled promises, the poor chalk this up to one more disappointment by nature of their poverty status.

The victim mindset says things like this:

- We are poor, and we are victims. We need help; we cannot do this on our own. There is something wrong with us. What do you have to give us? Dreams of tomorrow are too big; my stomach is loud. Do you have some food that will ease our suffering today?

- We are the exploited. We must be cautious, as the world is waiting to take advantage of us at any given time. We must hide what we have and what we are so others will not take advantage of us and steal what little we have.

- We have been taken advantage of before; we cannot help ourselves. We must repeat the stories of injustice to warn others from these abuses. We have an identity as a victim in a system of injustice. "I am a victim" is intrinsic to my identity, and since I have been victimized, I will always be a victim and a target for further victimizing.

- This victim needs some help! I depend on help from others since I am a victim. My life is spent in search of *survival* strategies and opportunities.

- Future investments are a waste of present resources and can easily be taken away. Do not risk eating today on a hope for tomorrow that can be swallowed up by a new disaster.

Five Stages of Dependence

1. Desperate-prideful-covering.
2. Humbled-receiving.
3. Humiliated-dependent.
4. Incapacitated-docile-receiving.
5. Dependent-resentful.

Resentful

In the worst cases, the poverty mindset becomes resentful of those assisting them while in their pervasive dependance mode. Those who possess more resources become a constant reminder to the poor of their lower estate and seeming inability to rise above it. Although they may be assisted in one or more areas through aid that reduces some of the discomfiture associated with poverty, they nonetheless remain in this state.

Why they cannot be "really helped" so that their condition changed from dependence to growth becomes the nagging question that builds even towards those who serve them through poverty programs, who either ignore or are oblivious to their circumstances that are the cause of the suffering. Resentment is bolstered by this thought, and the poor remain convinced that they could not ignore another person suffering so cavalierly as do those who either look down on or ignore them. This person will literally bite the hand that feeds them.

The goal is *moving people from poverty to wealth building*. Prolonged aid of any kind, no matter how well intended, creates and builds a dependency cycle that prevents sustainable growth, harms local businesses and wealth building capacity, and limits future expansion potential—if not killing it outright. Extreme caution must be used in providing aid that is not geared toward investment in increased capacity, expansion into new areas of enterprise and growth of existing crops, and materials being utilized for value-added products and services with higher market value than raw goods or materials.

We want to partner in sparking initiative and releasing potential. Empowerment after a crisis should move as quickly as possible from comfort and subsidy to building and growing, to avoid undermining healthy, progressive recovery and natural growth and expansion. Prolonged comfort and recovery will trap people in a cycle of dependance, and the comfort hoped for will lead to frustration and hopelessness.

3

Challenge

Existing Conditions, Analyze the System

POVERTY TENDS TO EXIST in a complex set of things: people, programs, patterns, behaviors, customs, cultures, leadership styles and systems, corruption, climate, resources, beliefs, history, rivalries, jealousies, inefficiencies, alliances, prejudices, assumptions, fiefdoms, governmental and intergovernmental relationships, business climates, trade patterns, access to markets, etc. Often these things are not working appropriately to empower and welcome growth and participation. The structures that are most essential to facilitate change tend to be the ones that are non-functional and the most intractable.

In the many areas of global poverty, there are some areas that take longer and are more intractable than others, such as government corruption, feudalism, cartels, lack of transportation, and so on. At this point many organizations take the route of determining what specific area they can address in isolation to the other intractable ones in hopes of making some change in some lives. These specialized projects target a single factor on its own with the hope of not being derailed by the corruption-fueled poverty system that is robbing these countries and communities of resources and opportunities. They then settle on a specific area, since "something must be done" after all.

PROBLEMATIC APPROACHES: TREATING SYMPTOMS OR CAUSES

Micro Solutions to Macro Systemic Problems

For example, if education is a problem but the government entity in charge cannot or will not be involved, an NGO will build, fund, and run a school for girls, only going to the government for the necessary building permits, etc. However, the parents are still too poor to pay school fees or feed their children. Part of a system is being addressed with significant resources, but the rest is being neglected, so it is like a rather large Band-Aid on a wounded system. The parents are still poor and reminded every day that someone from outside must care for their children since they cannot, furthering their sense of inability and incapacity.

These beliefs are not true; they simply lack the resources and tools to better themselves. If they have a hammer and wood, they will build a house. With seeds and land, they will grow a crop. But with food subsidy and "free education," they will build hopelessness and dependance accompanied by diminished dreams and eventual resentment.

Outside Control

All funding, leadership, and vision are determined by the outside organization. Even though a local manager may be hired, they will primarily fill out reports to satisfy the NGO and those who are giving grants to the NGO or charity.

"What is wrong with this solution?" one may ask. "We have identified that one of the problems is education, so we finally built a school that the government would not or could not build. That is a good thing." This decision likely came after many years of frustration and not too many small or medium-sized bribes and promised votes or actions by politicians, all to no avail.

Identifying a *Part* of the Problem: Sample Case Study

Identified Problem: Girls are dropping out of school at higher rates than boys.

Larger Problem/Source: Poverty and discrimination-assumed common causes by Westerners.

Solution 1: Educate girls; build a girls' school.

As an example, the lack of education for girls in the developing world may have a number of causes, not the least of which is local poverty and the inability of families to pay for all of their children to be educated. This generally gives preference to the boys, who will be expected to earn wages to support the families they will likely start at a young age. For many of the young girls, they would prefer to have children early and begin domestic life; likewise they do not want to burden their families with expenses for an education they perceive that *they do not need,* in order to have babies. Finally, who will get the water? Water? Most girls have this chore, and they spend hours a day hauling water for cooking, washing clothes, cleaning, etc.

Alternate Solution 2: Help parents earn enough to send their children to school.

The more wholistic solution would be for the families to be able to afford the school fees necessary for their own children, as opposed to being dependent on some unfamiliar outside charity that would fund education for a specified period. One way to accomplish this goal is strategizing *new medium-size businesses* as part of the project. These businesses can employ parents and stimulate the economy to create opportunities for sole proprietors to grow and engage in skills they already have or new ones, accompanied by a system to disciple people into this new identity of who they were made to be using their God-given gifts. This creates new potential and a mindset that can engage it effectively, "taking every thought captive" (2 Corinthians 10:5) that distracts from the good future that God has in mind for them.

Ongoing Outside Subsidies

Instead, aid money from outside sources is the dominant format, despite the fact that it is not a sustainable model and does not contribute to the economic expansion of the local community. Moreover, this model bypasses the local transformational leaders in the community, who have the greatest level of knowledge of what will and will not work in their community as well as the influence to bring about the economic and social transformation necessary. They are the visionary catalysts required, the motivators who keep things happening when everyone else has given up.

Crises, Corruption, Delays, Bribes, and Abuse

Many times, the attempt to leverage single-area solutions are borne out of two factors: first, the pressing weight of the ongoing problem, and second, the inefficiency of the government's role. The latter problem lies in the inability to get things going through the government agencies in charge or the extreme corruption and waste of resources when the government is involved, causing costs to raise upwards of 500 percent over what is necessary. Oftentimes foreign workers are brought in at wages ten to one hundred times those of local salaries, which is further exacerbated by notoriously high turnover rates by these expatriate expert employees.

Therefore, by the nature of these situations, many NGOs forge ahead in addressing single issues, like water wells, schools for girls, and so forth. But this is not the only solution path.

4

Wholistic Partnership Approaches and Strategies

How CAN WE CREATE systemic changes that are sustainable, replicable, locally led, and locally owned that result in continued expansion over time without getting mired in the mess of bribes, cartels, government corruption, etc.? Is that even possible? The answer is yes—it just takes a different approach.

OLD WAY: FOREIGN CONTROL

Why is a new way necessary, one may ask? We built our school, the girls are coming to the school, and therefore, everything is fine. Or is it? True long-term change that has continuous improvement, growth, and expansion takes time and leadership from the community itself. Too many people speak of community empowerment, but in reality, all the power resides with the NGO. There is no empowerment without power. Whoever has the money (owns the title to the land, controls all the money, and makes all the decisions) has the power.

Not Ours to Maintain

At this point it becomes a state where there is no real local control or local ownership of the project in the mind and spirit of the locals in the community. "This belongs to someone else," they will say. "Therefore, it is theirs to maintain and finance. We did not build these things. They were built by these outside organizations, schools, clinics, and retreat centers . . . If they were built by others, we have nothing to do with them. We were always excluded from the leadership."

No Plan or Budgeting for Local Control

Resources are doled out as specified by the dictates of the NGO's Washington, DC offices. Meanwhile, local initiatives for growth and expansion that could have funded the ongoing operation of these facilities are never considered, or at best are pushed aside as they do not meet the granting organization's funding parameters. Worse still, over time the funding will cease, and the outside entities' school or well will fail, as there is no source for local funding through economic expansion, new businesses, or improved agricultural practice. Exclusively "foreign funded" operations inevitably close because they are burdened by the weight of their own design, based on western standards and practices. This combines with the inability of a financially weak and impoverished community's unimproved capacity to carry such a heavy load when its capacity was not expanded along with the building of the school or whatever the case may be.

SYSTEMIC SOLUTIONS

So, what is the solution? We must address the systemic and specific problems in a more wholistic way that is locally led and economically empowered and responsible if we want to see sustainability. That is, we need complex solutions to complex problems. We must prayerfully follow the leading of God's Spirit in uncharted territories of trust and faithfulness. Likewise, as we trust and follow, we must find workarounds for the things beyond our control, like corrupt governments or officials, bad roads, rainy seasons, etc. We can do this by innovating and creating new models that ultimately take all of these variables into account without resorting to jaded frustration or forcing partial solutions that are unsustainable in the long run.

Learn the Local Language of Blessing: Boys and Teens

Road Repair

Phillip wanted to see more trade in his village near Bamenda, but a poor road filled with potholes off the highway kept traffic and customers away. He pleaded with the government for two years. Then he took a dozen soccer balls to the community and told the boys and teens that once they filled the potholes, they would get the soccer balls. The boys filled the potholes in one weekend, and then they celebrated over a meal and enjoyed some soccer.

This is an excellent example of leverage. The wage and work for filling the potholes was higher than the reward of a soccer ball in monetary terms. However, in terms of group enjoyment, the dreams of playing with a real inflated soccer ball, as opposed to balls of discarded strings and pieces of rope wrapped in old tape, put a smile on their faces with each kick of the ball. This later led to starting a driving school so the older teens could find employment and earn a living. Good work, Phillip!

Learn the Language: Government

Doing things in new ways and empowering local resources requires a humbler stance from those with the outside financial resources. We all need local expertise and outside assistance to achieve great goals.

Get Help

I have helped people get building permits in the United States after the city had told them *no* and given them reasons. However, accompanying them to the office and asking a few questions about other potential options, how the local governmental systems and priorities worked, and how they themselves might be able to suggest we can get the project completed has always resulted in approval of a building permit. The owners are often amazed as if they just watched a magic trick, but there is no magic. I and others have learned their language and culture through trial and error, so we are able to get answers and forge solutions.

I have stood in line and witnessed many builders and architects with elaborate plans castigate those behind the counter, only to be sent away with a long list of things to do and little hope of success on their next visit, because they have made an enemy of the person assisting them instead of an ally. This happens most often when people lead with what they know and demand their rights! Instead, one can lead with questions and seek solutions, which if they are not within the law can be quietly challenged with another question, "Doesn't the code say this? How does that apply in this case?"

Learn the Language: Medical

The same is true of the medical field. As I was in the ICU with a very distraught father, the doctors and nurses said they were going to need permission to intubate his three-year-old son. The child's rare chemical burn reaction to a medicine he had taken (Stevens-Johnson Syndrome) would soon migrate to the boy's lungs, and once they were swollen, it would not be possible to insert the intubation tube into the lungs. With the father there, I began asking a series of questions about the course of care and whether the doctor had worked on a case like this before.

He informed us that he was in fact the unofficial, unpublished expert in treating this condition (Stevens-Johnson) globally and had just finished a case for a girl in China that he treated with her doctors via the Web. As we asked more questions, the doctor asked us, "Do you want to see the pictures of the response to treatment?" He then wheeled a chair over to the computer terminal in the ICU room and brought up images of a young lady with burns just like my friend's child. He went through the pictures showing the stages of irritation all the way through the condition subsiding over the course of months.

Months later I was in the father's office, celebrating many miracles of God's blessing and providence, when he mentioned a difficulty with insurance reimbursements that was causing him to owe $240,000. Wince. I had worked in medical billing and insurance in the past and had recently encountered similar challenges in my daughters' billings. So, I walked him through the process of speaking to the hospital's billing department, the insurance company's claims resolution departments, and how they all coordinated. He later reported to me that almost all of the debt had been eliminated through this process.

Listen and Learn

We need to speak the language of the experts to learn how we can get what we need. When we come as the experts due to our resource status, we are relegated to a ghetto of our own understanding and perpetually frustrated that the locals do not adequately understand our good intentions or needs. As we have seen, a new way of thinking is required to listen and learn effectively.

Essential Element II

Empowering Local Change Agents

Globally Exposed and Educated Leaders

5

Expanding and Releasing Creativity

DREAMING: VISION POTENTIAL

Learn and Empower

GOD HAS GIVEN EXTRAORDINARY creativity and understanding to leaders in every community. In the following chapters, we will see how we can *learn from and empower* local leaders to do things we never imagined possible. We can take the passion that drives us to see things improved in what are desperate circumstances, by empowering the creativity, knowledge, and understanding of those who are positioned to lead the change and transformation in a community well into the future.

Harnessing Local Creativity

By nature, we want to change things and make them better. From our earliest years, we move our feet through the sand at the beach, and then we begin to move it intentionally and purposefully as our inborne desire to build and expand is released. We get buckets and add water and then shape the sand with the same buckets; we create turrets where we can launch our attacks, or create our defenses, or as a place to look for our true love to rescue us.

EXTRAORDINARY OPPORTUNITY

Strategic Targeted Investment

When a problem is manifest, handing out a little bit of money rarely solves the problem. It may make us feel good and or alleviate the guilt of a Western visitor or friend, but the long-term problems remain. Ironically, if these small donations are continued long enough, the handing out of money can distract people from genuine, lasting, wholistic, and expansive multiplying solutions, instead unintentionally creating a class of weak-minded and sycophant dependence among the locals. This is a path away from formative solutions.

When this happens, the most creative entrepreneurial leaders will be bypassed. The best and brightest who could be building, growing, and expanding instead lead the way in holding our "talented hands of organizational solutions" in anticipation of another small transfer payment that will not even provide enough for the survival of the family. They will work to maintain good relations with each other in hopes that the relationship may one day bring meaningful and lasting solutions to the intractable problems.

For most, though, the hoped-for pipeline of creativity and strategic investment has never been built. In its place, they watch the skyline waiting for care and aid to arrive from heaven, pushed out of the back of a plane too afraid to even land. These exclusively outside-oriented approaches fail time and again, operating from a constant-crisis mode, while at the same time ignoring the local talent and resources that are already on the ground waiting to be developed.

When given the necessary tools for what they need in order to harness and develop the local resources that they have within their own community, the crisis begins to abate as productive multiplication is enabled. Why are they stuck in the first place? They simply lack the capital and resource knowhow to move forward. Instead, the vast local human resources wither away in a valley of dry bones while well-meaning poverty donators visit the "poor people" who "cannot care for themselves" and dole out one more tip.

DIVINE INVESTMENT

No one wants to be poor, and God does not create people to be poor. On the contrary, all human beings and the communities they belong to have enormous, untapped resources of vision and talent. Not only are these God-given resources just waiting to be released and flourish, but they also have the potential to create a more dynamic world than we ever imagined.

Yet, the current practice of even the most benevolent of those in the West and the developed world is to make regular transfer payments that leave this vast resource of billions of people under the tyranny of low expectations and wildly limited, under-resourced opportunities. We are building shacks over gold mines and deeming it good. We are erecting huts over diamonds in the rough and ignoring the gems that will not only bless their own communities but the world.

This is where many may bring up all the reasons why developing nations cannot see progress and how much greed and corruption is involved. Ironically, poverty alleviation efforts almost always rely on these same corrupt systems or exclude local community leaders with the necessary abilities and cultural awareness, resulting in ineffective solutions in the end.

A recent advertisement for a well-known charity emphasized that they could not alleviate world poverty, but they could use your money to help one child. *Why?* Of course, there is nothing wrong with helping a child. In fact, helping a child is a worthy and good thing. Transforming a community is an even better thing. Fostering the creation of a creativity-releasing and vitality-producing community—where people use their abilities to wholistically grow and prosper and where parents feed their own children, instead of an institution—is a better measure of success than how many poor children belly up to the table at another institution.

By training and equipping global leaders who are studying in the United States to return to their communities and transform them, we have learned how to assist in designing sustainable models for funding local ministries and community transformation since 2007. We are helping to bring in a kingdom-hearted return on the original divine investment in these leaders.

6

Count the Cost
Understanding Real Costs and Alternatives

CONSIDER FOR A MOMENT the cost of feeding 10,000 children. By "cost" I don't just mean the money, although it is significant and the thing that most Westerners consider first. But what would it involve to feed 10,000 children every day? Three times a day, meaning 30,000 meals? How big of a kitchen would you need? How big would the hall be where they are fed?

One of my daughters attended USC with over 50,000 students. They do not attempt to feed them all in a single location; the logistics are just too difficult.

LOGISTICS

Feeding 10,000 children would require multiple shifts of children coming through the food lines and being seated, and then moving them out while the next group was preparing to take their seats. And given the amount of time it would take to serve 10,000 children, one would not need 10,000 seats at the same time, as many seats would empty as the massive, endless line snaked along. In all likelihood, the line would stay all day as breakfast would run into the noontime meal and then the evening meal.

So, perhaps we should have regional feeding centers to reduce the congestion. That may help, but we have yet to explore the kitchen requirements for this vast number of meals, the refrigeration required, as well as the loading docks to receive the semi-trucks full of food that would be arriving hourly. Once we have figured all of this out, we have yet to fund it. What will it cost for all of this infrastructure just to build it and get it ready to go? How much staff will be needed for preparation, cooking, serving, and janitorial staff to clean the kitchen and dining halls? This revenue-negative enterprise will cost tens of thousands of dollars a day to run in human resource and materials.

Questions:

- Is this idea well intended? *Yes.*
- Is it doable? *Possibly.*
- Can donors be found to support it? *Possibly.*
- Is it sustainable? *Not without many donors, long term.*
- Is it potentially self-sustaining? *Not as presented; it is a dependency model.*
- Can it naturally expand and multiply to other communities through local support? *No.*
- Is this ministry or activity creating self-sufficiency or dependence? *Dependence . . .*

DONATION-AND-TRANSFER-PAYMENTS CYCLE

Much of the work of the church is achieved by donation and transfer. Donations are requested and made, and then those donations are given as payments to others. Interestingly, we do not tend to look at the source of those donations. Where did the money for these donations come from that go to do missions and bring aid to those who are suffering? What activities did we do that supply the donations? Is it a car wash, candy sale, wages and income from businesses and investments? The same thing that raised money in the West is what will fund opportunities in the majority world: employment, salaries, and profit through businesses.

Aid Models

The above model for feeding 10,000 children that we just explored is an *aid-based* model. Outside resources and leadership come to address a local problem. Unfortunately, and all too often, natural systems of family nurture and table time together are supplanted by well-meaning attempts at assuaging local deficiencies in food security, education, or medical care due to the economic capacity of parents. Programs such as orphanages and free meals to alleviate a single particular problem in an area or community create new challenges that strain at the social fabric and inadvertently harm families. The hunger issue is addressed, but the holistic needs of the community are not addressed with sustainable, systemic solutions, and many new problems will be created and exacerbated by the intrusion of this proposed feeding machine. But the children need food! Yes, of course they do, but urgency and expediency have many unwanted offspring, like inefficiency, dependency, loss of parental roles and nurture, and so on.

Let us not rush to substitute one set of problems with another. May we instead work diligently and prayerfully in cooperative partnership with transformational local leaders who are equipped and empowered to lead within local communities to bring about dreamed-of transformations. This requires relational investment over the course of years to build trust between leaders and communities and to leverage the God-given resources and opportunities that exist for both.

7

When Helping Is Discipleship

MAKING DISCIPLES

Discipleship in the West is practiced most often as a series of classes taught in a church building. Jesus' disciples walked with him, ate with him, and were apprentices in healing and casting out demons as they went down the road together from community to community, taking breaks, breaking bread, and having discussions. When large groups gathered to see Jesus' miracles, the disciples had their assignments as the gospel was shared and baptisms performed.

When we live life together, performing the regular functions of our lives in the midst of physical work, our character, work habits, and patience (or lack thereof) are revealed. Conversations spill forth, from the polite and planned to the personal and passionate struggles we all face. This is the inroad to life change on the highway of life.

Life on Life

Working with Shane on a construction project, a particular hobby of mine, allowed *us* to have a much more effective discipleship relationship. (Notice I did not say discipleship *program*.) Working together breaks down many barriers and exposes our true strengths and weaknesses, and this is simply not possible in the artifice of a classroom, in an academic setting, or in a church building. The gifts, knowledge, and relatability of the environment is the meat of the discipleship process, and we are laid bare by our activity as to how we think and process and accomplish various tasks. Our level of patience is revealed, as well as the particular things that we enjoy or that frustrate us. In this environment, dialogue and questions naturally flow from between parties.

Discipleship is best when it is on-the-job training in close proximity with the parties involved. It is life on life, walking together, driving together, where both are learning, where both are teaching. There is a natural push and pull, but there is still a clear leader.

LEARNING, LISTENING, OVERCOMING DIFFERENCES

When working cross culturally—whether there are generational differences or cultural differences of nationality, language, and custom—we are learning from each other about what we value, what motivates us for change, and the obstacles our unique places in the world and time create that hinder achieving these objectives.

In the classroom, a line of information can be transmitted, from teacher to learner and back to the teacher if there is an effective loop of communication that is taking the experience to a higher level. But in the hands-on activities of life described in Deuteronomy 6—in settings outside those four walls of the classroom—we get clearer glimpses of how we communicate and transfer faith. Life is displayed and the learning is integrated along with the character that is being formed as we live life together.

What does all of this have to do with development? Leaders in the West as well as those in the developing world need to form strong ties of trust and mutual appreciation. Simply moving money does not accomplish the high goals we all desire.

While local leaders are working with a community to add to its growth capacity, new jobs and new businesses are created. New relationships and training are performed by local leaders integrating new people into new opportunities. *These are all future disciple-making opportunities with transformational potential, personally, corporately, and spiritually.*

As we build relationships of trust, accountability, and discipleship, we create a culture for all those who will follow in our partnerships in both locations; this is the mind and will of Christ Jesus for us together.

For too long we have been willing to subordinate the use of our mutual gifts and resultant mutual blessings to each other, and instead substituted specialized, distant organizations to conduct the transfer of money on our behalf, instead of real-life relationships and experiences that give each of us hope, passion, and purpose.

This is the stuff we were created for. People long to be ambassadors of change, and that is clearly manifest in our times through the protests of social justice groups filled with people teeming to make a difference in the world. Yet these same people often lack effective leadership to channel their abilities, dreams, and aspirations into tangible, creative methods of engagement that will bring about the kind of change they desire. Instead they are subordinated to government structures that are incapable of the creative life-on-life engagement that Jesus modeled.

SAMPLE CONVERSATION

We were laying out string lines to level a foundation that we were digging for a new structure. "Have you heard the Bible verse, 'The stone the builders rejected has become the cornerstone'?" I asked. Then I proceeded onward:

"In Jesus' time they took the best, most perfect square stone, and it became the first one for the most prominent corner. This stone became the reference point for everything else in the structure; everything else had to align with it, or by definition it was out of alignment. In this way the building would be square, and the walls straight and erect. If the cornerstone was not straight, the whole building would be deformed and disformed in accordance with the misalignments of the cornerstone. Each successive stone or element would then amplify the imperfections of the cornerstone, resulting in a distinctly misshaped structure.

"Since we are using concrete and not actual stones for our foundation, we need to use a metal construction square from the hardware store." I then pointed to the swimming pool in the yard and had Shane stand in one corner and look straight ahead.

"What do you see?" I called out to him.

"The pool is not straight," he said. The pool appeared to be in a rectangular shape, but it was in fact out of square.

You see, the young man who set the stakes made an error in his measurements and never checked it with a square, so the entire pool was out of square. This was the supervisor's first swimming pool as a supervisor, and he missed a step. He didn't check his measurements with a square. He assumed his measurements from the fence were accurate and square. He never checked them to confirm if the information he was trusting was accurate.

Out of this simple example in real life, a long conversation flowed with laughter about our errors and mistakes. I often wonder what information I am taking in that is not accurate. What are your sources of information? Which ones rule over the others? Which ones have let you down? You want to be sure when you are starting out not to make a monument to your youth and inexperience by missing steps. Always be ready to ask for help and check things out to avoid costly errors.

DEFINITIONS

Disciple making is bringing someone along a path to become something. In the building and construction trades, this is often called an apprenticeship. Discipling is most effectively achieved through watching and learning and doing with a leader, or disciple maker. Do the thing you do together. Tell the story of your bakery, how it works, how it was formed, what has worked, what you struggle with, how your people are influenced for the gospel in your business, how you pray for them, love them, and lead them with integrity as a boss, co-worker, manager, or whatever your role may be.

A *discipline*, in an academic setting, refers to a field of study or topic, subject matter, an academic major, or endeavor in the subject matter. All of these are referred to as part of the discipline.

LEARNING AS A DISCIPLE

Learning a specific skill or job requires adherence to the subject matter and learning in a holistic, immersive environment. None of these environments is perfect, and depending on the discipline learned, it usually takes months to years to acquire a functional level of expertise or greater. Along the way come the skills that accompany the discipline and will continue to grow and ultimately bring benefits congruent with a lifetime of learning and practice.

Long-term relationships between leaders require significant personal investment. In this way we can look out for each other, pray for each other, and find resources and compassionate, loving encouragement to cover for weaknesses we all have. Likewise, we can challenge each other to greater heights in our ministries and personal lives. Instead of spending our time asking "why?" about every problem, our solution-inspired friends will impel us toward renewed vision and passion that says, "Why not!"

Jesus discipled people in different ways than traditional Western churches or missionaries tend to functionally operate. The environments we now use for what is called disciple making in the church, which is the mandate of the Great Commission in Matthew 28:18–20, are almost exclusively based in informational transfer in the classroom learning environments, which echo the modern university system with lecturers and students.

SEPARATION OF WORK AND VALUES/BELIEFS

Western thinking is highly influenced by a culture of efficiency, specialization, and production to the highest number of people at the lowest cost, in order to produce wealth. Another influence is a legal history emphasizing equal opportunity that is practiced in the U.S. as a separation of church and state. This separation and specialization principle has migrated to separating ministries within a church by age and interest of people.

In commerce we separate business and personal development into isolated, unrelated categories. Many people act on this separating principle in their removal of personal values and beliefs from the workplace—as if this was possible. Beliefs are then relegated to a particular place of worship or spiritual encounter, but they are viewed as separate from what it takes to run a business.

Can right beliefs equal good business practices? This may seem like a scary step of comingling things that we have decided culturally to separate, trusting the experts without any proof of ability or results. Can our faith and work life be integrated in a *holistic* and winsome manner?

"I do not want to be sued," one may say. "I cannot force my religion on someone where I work." That is true; however, that is not the objective. Instead we can have an open discussion about our values, and how they drive the values we pursue in our workplace. To keep things open and dialogical, ask the person you are working with if they understand the values in operation with the work environment, and keep things open enough that they can tell you about their beliefs and what motivates them. This process of "give and take" creates enormous openness if applied from a genuine heart.

WHAT DOES THIS MEAN?

Many Christian workers are focused on one-time evangelism as an outcome of sharing a gospel presentation about repentance and forgiveness of sin through Jesus Christ. Jesus' mandate was that we make disciples, which is a holistic process including a point of decision to follow Christ that can occur at different places in the discipleship process. For many the *a priori* question is "How do we get people to become followers of Jesus Christ?" Only subsequent to that conversion do we begin making disciples.

Disciple making is a pathway that includes the goal of evangelism, but its process and focus is not as exclusivist to a momentary, specific decision as it is to a lifelong following in the way of Jesus. Indeed, it refers to a total lifestyle guided by values and beliefs that transform your character and cause your work to be in alignment to the one whose image you are modeling within the discipleship relationship.

After serving as a pastor among different Asian and African and Middle Eastern communities, I have observed that many young converts to the faith enter through service in the community to those who are suffering in the world. People are now asking, "What is the difference your faith or religion makes in the world?" Long before they consider joining the faith, they will join the justice, compassion, counseling, and caring works to see if the root beliefs result in worthy action and compatible community life.

One high school student came to the church to perform community service hours packing shoe boxes with presents for Operation Christmas Child, an initiative of Samaritan's Purse that gives presents to children all over the world in poor communities. Later he became involved with other youths in the church and also served with them. After some months, he made a commitment to Jesus Christ. It is not our job to determine the order of things; we must follow God's ordering as led by the Spirit, and then join in what God is doing.

Clarifications

After the ministry team comes and the preacher shares the gospel and many people make commitmentsto Jesus Christ, there is the short-term and lifelong task of making disciples. Both of these aspects ensure that these recent commitments are not lost as in the Parable of the Sower that Jesus told in Matthew 13. We would do well to follow the example that Jesus set for his disciples and invite people to come and follow us in life together, as we follow Christ outside the church building as well as inside.

People will come forward, raise a hand, and get baptized, and they are often called converts. But there are others left after the evangelistic rally is over. Some are curious but unconvinced for now. Others are waiting to see if the change in other people's lives is real, and still others never even made it to the "event" and are disinterested in a God who may or may not love them when they do not even have a job to take care of their family. All of them need a life touch and an opportunity to live the disciple's life at whatever stage they are in.

HOLISTIC ENGAGEMENT

When we engage with a poor community so that they can achieve growth and utilize the gifts in each individual to their greatest potential, we will be engaging those who would not come to a church meeting but are interested in a job. Along the way they then become curious and interested in the God who helped them get a job, and they feel the kind of productivity and reward of providing for and blessing others that is built into all people by God.

Aid or Job?

Giving someone a bag of rice will fill their stomach for a few days; it is an act of momentary compassion with very short-term, locally unsustainable results. But it does not engage the natural creativity and productivity inherent in people that must be facilitated or harvested so that they feel whole, alive, and purposeful. That is why Jesus said, "Go and make disciples," and that is what we are doing here and around the world through community transformation.

The Bible teaches us all of these things—to preach the gospel (Matthew 28:18), to feed the poor (Matthew 25:34–40), and to work (1 Thessalonians 4:11). In the West, we know the value of work, but when we engage the local or global poor, we often ignore their need for dignity and work, and thereby exclude them from being in a position to help others when in a season of need. This also excludes them from help finding a way out and supporting themselves and blessing others in a continual cycle. What we tend to think is "Well, there are no jobs here, so I will just send them some money." This decision is quick and easy, but it can be deadly in the long term to people whom we are called to help up, not just help out for the short term.

Vision

To remind you of the vision that was shared in the introduction, I implore you to consider undertaking the following work that is both challenging and fruitful:

- Foster environments where jobs, careers, businesses, and industries can be created in a given community.

- Partner with the creative entrepreneurial people in that community.

- Equip local managers for long-term success to run these businesses and industries.

- Do all of this with the goal of giving the glory to God.

Essential Element III

Thinking in New Ways

Support, Follow, and Listen to the Local Leaders

8

Listening to the Experts

A RESPONSE TO *WHEN HELPING HURTS*

YOU MAY HAVE HEARD of the 2009 book *When Helping Hurts* by Steve Corbett and Brian Fikkert. In this chapter, we will investigate the individual steps proposed by the authors in an effort to find a better way at arriving at legitimate solutions. The premise of their book is that much of the movement of monies from the West to the poorer parts of the world has not brought about the desired overall improvement; often by creating dependency cycles, it has undermined its goals. In fact, research suggests it has often had unintended ill effects on many local economies, businesses, and the ability of people to produce their own goods locally.

One can definitely display correlative graphs that have an inverse relationship between declining GDP (gross domestic product, or the economic output of a country) and increased aid. Aid goes up; GDP goes down. But as previously stated, aid as simple transfer payments is the problem, and not the solution being proposed here.

The pathway out of poverty is the goal of business expansion in local communities as well as specific businesses that are established by local entrepreneurs to fund local charities through their long-term profits. These businesses must be led by transformational leaders with exposure to alternative options. On the inverse, long-term aid is the noose around the neck of poor economies and does little more than prop up corrupt governments that gorge themselves on the aid dollars before they trickle down to the empty hands poor, if they ever make it at all. The majority of this book focuses on what Corbett and Fikkert cover in two pages of their book,[1] namely, the key to productivity in the projects that we have worked with over and over.

Corbett and Fikkert write about "business as mission" (BAM):

> BAM is not for everyone. Many churches and missionaries are not gifted at running businesses. Moreover, even a person who is gifted at operating a business in North America will not necessarily be successful at doing so in a Majority World country. The culture and business climate in some contexts may make North American Business not completely transferrable. The Promotion, Partnership, and Complementary training models are all much simpler to pursue than BAM, thereby reducing the risk of harm.[2]

One of our values is that the pastor should not run the business. North Americans are not running the businesses; rather local businesspeople are running them without operational subsidy. Finally, even though Corbett and Fikkert's "Promotion, Partnership, and Complementary" models may be "much simpler to pursue" according to the authors, they do not bring about the robust economic expansion that medium-sized businesses do. The harm is in exclusively relegating people to tiny ventures on minuscule budgets with no opportunity for leveraging economic expansion and potentially hiring others as employees with higher wages.

Microfinance has helped many people move out of desperate poverty and is certainly an area of expertise and practice that we partner with, but it is not our primary focus, as it stalls quickly in business multiplication and is slow at creating wealth in the community.

---

1. Corbett and Fikkert, *When Helping Hurts*, 198–99.
2. Corbett and Fikkert, *When Helping Hurts*, 198.

PARTNERING FOR DEVELOPMENT[3]—OUR PROCESS

Step 1: Identifying Problems

The Premise: Aid Fails

Unfortunately, many readers of *When Helping Hurts* mistakenly take from it that Western *participations* in poverty relief should be all but eliminated, since they are not doing the good intended, but instead are doing harm. Now, this is a vast oversimplification of the book; however, I am not speaking just to specific or actual content but rather the reactions and perceptions that flow from various interactions with majority-world friends.

I have encountered a number of people who are aware of the book and claim to have read it (or at least know someone who did), but they state that identifying a problem is only the first step towards solving it. The problem is not specifically the movement of money from the developed world to the developing world; the problem is the form and path that the money takes, that is, as aid subsidies rather than specific, business-multiplying, economic investment and job creation.

How It Happens: Failure to Seek Wise Counsel Locally

How often do we ask local people what they need to improve their situation? Aid organizations, NGOs, and governments regularly go into communities and make observations and analysis and determine what needs to be done. This process usually circumvents local people and leaders, or they reluctantly go along with a proffered solution because at least some resource will come their way even though it is not what they really need, and perhaps it will open a relationship to later getting what they really need.

This is the problem and inefficiency of top-down, one-size-fits-all solutions by resource-rich experts that fail time and again. These "experts" are structurally and culturally unprepared to listen and partner in an egalitarian, participatory partnership, instead of an authoritarian, implementor role. Please, *listen to the locals*. Take some time and have some tea together.

---

3. Corbett and Fikkert, *When Helping Hurts*, 241.

Making the Problem Worse: Experts and Info

When operating in a so-called "expert mode" because one can identify a problem, we tend to conflate the problem along with the data and the general practices and plans that we are tied to. So, if we have increased aid as stated and decreasing GDP, and if we conflate that data and thereby conclude that moving money to these countries is the problem, we now will wrongly perceive both giving aid money and investing in business and development as a cause of the problem.

Is It the Amount of Money Or Its Pathway and Uses?

But the question is: How are we deploying the money after it has been given? And equally important, what is its pathway and how does that affect the amount that makes it to the poor in the first place? We must realistically identify if the money is going through corrupt governments, only to be pilfered, and then the remaining amount is distributed as food aid.

This same money could just as well be directly invested in medium-sized businesses as well as other local businesses, schools, clinics, and improved agricultural practices. All these things must be led by local, transformed leaders and governing boards who manage the resources and grow them without external control. If there is no promise of ongoing subsistence funding, then accountability for local growth and expansion depends on the local leaders for local success.

So then, that logic of aid being the primary problem may not hold. It is rather the application, type of aid, and the pathway of the aid or outside resources that is the issue. Applying the correct solution to the correct problem is a skill and an artform.

Identify the Real Problem

If I have a leaky roof, I need to patch the hole where the water is entering. Simple. If I apply several patches, I may determine that the roof needs replacement. So far this sounds logical, and many a roofer has made money this way. What if the roof still leaks? The patch may well have been good, but *only* if it was in the right place. There may be only one small leak. Yet, a thousand patches can be unsuccessfully placed on the roof if it is not on the point of origin of where the water is entering. We then have an ugly patchwork of useless "solutions" that may themselves lead to more problems just by their presence. (Talk to a qualified roofer and they will explain the rest.)

Listen to the Experienced Local Experts with Proven Results

Some years back, I had a home in Indiana hit by golf ball-size hail and larger. Fifty thousand homes in the community had to have their rooves replaced, including mine. My roof was steep with a lot of gables, except for a small, flat stretch of roof over the front porch.

The roofer asked if the front porch leaked. I said no. His reply was, "Leave it alone if it does not leak."

As a first-time homeowner of a brand-new house, I was emphatic: If I was getting a new roof, I wanted a new roof for the whole house. So, he put a new flat roof over the old one as I requested, against his advice . . . and it leaked. He came to fix it four times, and it kept on leaking. The small porch ceiling light fixture filled with water, stains were appearing on the brick siding, the warranty ran out, and the roofer went back to Texas. Finally, I removed all the old roofing and the plywood underneath it. I placed the rafters at a steeper angle and installed a new roof that was like the original one. And it did not leak.

I should have listened to the expert.

Good Intentions Can Have Bad Results

I am indebted to the observations and creative solutions of the local leaders who practice in this area and their findings. They taught me the principles that I teach and apply in projects. For example, "the pastor should not run the businesses" that will support the ministries they were founded to support. Why? I was told that pastors running businesses tend to go bankrupt.

Here is why. Pastors have big hearts and tend to conflate the business practices with the ministry practices. They are here to give. So, if they are in the egg business, a person comes to the pastor and says, "I really need some eggs, but I have no money." The pastor, being the pastor at heart, gives them some eggs, and before long all the eggs are gone—along with the profits, jobs, and the business.

The Business Is Not a Charity. . .

A ministry is a ministry, and a business is a business. If a pastor is attempting to run a business, this separation between the ministry and a supporting business will be unclear; instead the supporting business will begin to appear as a charity or ministry, since that is what pastors are called to run. Our model of transforming poverty necessitates hiring qualified managers who are selected by the local board to run the businesses, and the managers are replaced if there is not a reasonable profit. Hiring is not a charitable act; it is a purposeful act.

The business is not a charity. It is a business whose profits support a local charity to make it sustainable. Likewise it is employing people from the community, which is also a blessing. Therefore, its profits are essential for the salaries of workers and their families that it supports as well as the needs of the charity to continue to function.

The fact that pastors make poor business leaders does not mean there should be no local businesses to support charities like schools and clinics. Learn from the mistakes of others, keep the pastor out of the business and in the ministry, but do not throw out the opportunity for business just because pastors tend not to have the aptitude to run them.

So, as we have learned from others who have worked in missions and local leaders who are serving in their communities, we have gleaned essential principles and practices that build on the observations of others, and sometimes seem to contradict them but are merely being approached from a different angle. Our contributions build on the research they have done, although our practice and expertise is not in research itself, but in the practical outworking of sustainable business models to fund specific ministries and create an environment for economic expansion.

The application of transformative models that achieve the longest-term results will accompany exponential and fruitful growth strategies empowering local leaders and those they influence and raise up to transform regions and countries.

When Helping Hurts rightly points out the damage caused by transfer payments from wealthy nations to impoverished nations (in the form of food, clothing, and other subsistence or monetary payments, or through investments in church buildings, wells, and subsidizing microfinance) indeed fosters a dependency cycle. The net effect of these transfer payments has contributed to the net GDP of the recipient constituent countries declining in an almost identical correlative curve that tracks with the increase of *transfer payments*. (Note: The term "transfer payments" is regularly used here because the word "aid" does not delineate between short-term, essential disaster relief assistance and long-term subsidies in caring for the poor. Aid is called aid whether in the "relief form" after a natural disaster or aid as ongoing "life subsidies" for a prolonged period—whether it actually aids people to a more prosperous, self-sustaining life or not.)

MAJORITY-WORLD REACTIONS TO *WHEN HELPING HURTS*

Among my Asian and African partners and friends, Corbett and Fikkert's book comes off as offensive, because they perceive its message to be that Africa, Asia, and other poor regions should not receive any assistance or aid, and that efforts to alleviate the grinding poverty they experience should cease. I do not believe that is the authors' purpose or intent. But when someone is from a poor region and the only trickle of resources to alleviate this poverty is seemingly encouraged to withdraw by another seemingly arrogant Westerner—who appears not to have sought the counsel of those they are speaking for—it can seem callous and thoughtless. When your only current lifeline is seemingly threatened with being severed, without any apparent thought or hope of replacement, the general anxiousness that causes to those who are on the receiving end of the lifeline can be well understood.

This perception is ironic, though, since Fikkert now directs significant educational efforts through Chalmers.org for development work training for local congregations and culture-specific resources for the developing world, which are overall very good, with a few glaring exceptions. The major deficiency lies in the area of BAM, or "business as mission," which is a major focus of this book. Michael Bamwesigye Badriaki, in his book *When Helping Works*, takes the authors to account in many more areas and is recommended reading to get a glimpse of a majority-world perspective. His comments are prescient and largely on point, questioning Corbett and Fikkert's "best practices" that they say churches regularly violate.[4] The points Badriaki makes about the continued emphasis of Western givers and others as receivers is one argued

---

4. Badriaki, *When Helping Works*, xvi; cf. Corbett and Fikkert, *When Helping Hurts*, 14.

against throughout this work. If one cannot see the place that those in the majority world have to give to the West and the areas where the West has to learn, the system is out of balance.

My place here is not to sit in judgment but to serve as a reporter of the perceptions of people from different places in the world as we work to build our mutual understandings and goals of alleviating unnecessary suffering in Jesus' name. My hope is that we may give birth to a more just society that reflects our calling. "He has told you, O man, what is good; and what does the Lord require of you but to do justice, and to love kindness, and to walk humbly with your God?" (Micah 6:8). We are all on this earth together, and we would do well to listen intelligently and speak carefully, while retaining our passion for the peoples of the world.

Here are the remaining steps similar to those outlined in *When Helping Hurts* modified with additional refining questions, which have proven effective for our global partners over the years.

Step 2: Identifying Solutions

Questions:

- Who are the local stake holders? Have they been included in the process?

- Are the solutions being developed in cooperation with other local leaders who have had the opportunity to observe multiple models, both within and outside their respective communities?

- Are we working with creative entrepreneurs, or managers, or both?

- Is there a way this solution can be implemented initially on a smaller scale to prove the efficacy and local acceptance of the idea?

- What local resources have been identified, including skills, natural resources, etc.?

- Can this idea or solution be scaled to surrounding communities? Is this being done in a way that supports and develops local leaders and local control and ownership?

Step 3: Implementing Solutions

Questions:

- Is there good feedback and support for our pioneering leader?
- What does their personal support network look like? How are we praying through solutions, miracles, and provision?
- Are funds being handled in a way that brings honor and trust, while limiting mishandling?
- Are we achieving our established goals from our business model?

Step 4: Refining Solutions

Questions:

- Are we willing to make necessary changes, including realigning relationships with influencers that may not be working out at this time?
- Is there adequate progress in our business model to go forward?
- What changes will get us on track or keep us there?
- Do we have the right people in the right positions, based on efficacy and performance, not politics and preference?
- What are the new ideas coming up from the success of this endeavor, and how we can support them?

Step 5 (*Our Added Step): Multiplication of the Solution Through Practitioners

Questions:

- Who is being mentored that can lead this locally in the future or multiply it in a neighboring community?
- By year three, who have we begun to mentor that will reproduce this solution in another community in year five?
- What are our expectations for emerging new leaders? How are they being discipled? What are the characteristics we need to see practiced by them to be ready to launch and lead a project?

Overall, success in the modified process suggested above combines *creatives* and their ability to imagine as well as *managers* and their ability to bring stability and accountability.

9

Unhealthy Attachments
When Self-Serving Leaders Seek to Join

NOTE ON LOCAL LEADERSHIP TEAMS DISRUPTION

BY THE TIME STEPS 2–5 from the previous chapter are being implemented, there is a tendency for unhealthy leaders to become attached to the project for their own personal benefit or that of an existing ministry that they lead. This type of leader will start to have a detrimental effect that the project leader will often not see or will minimize. This is often due to their prior existing relationship and the significant impact that this person has had in their lives.

Two things occur in this situation simultaneously.

First, there is an ongoing disruption that this leader is causing among those being helped. The disruptor will assert their authority or act in various ways that are distracting, self-serving, beyond their capacity, and makes promises that are ultimately not fulfilled. These actions may appear to be wildly supportive, but because this person is unable to perform on their promises, they will only bring disrepute to the overall project.

Second, there is a sense of guilt by our local creative leader, who feels that to intervene would be to show disrespect to this troublesome leader whom they want to honor. Honor can be shown most effectively in acknowledging those who have helped and influenced without giving them the microphone or platform where they fail.

How Do We Know If We Are Dealing with This Kind of Person?

The initial stages are harder to identify, as the requests and personal insertions will be less obviously self-serving and instead will appear to be supportive and participatory. But as time goes on, there will begin to emerge a multifaceted pattern of public grandiosity, unkept and unkeepable promises, and "volunteering" that pushes aside rising disciples in order to place themselves closer to funding representatives. In offering "honest critiques" of the leader, the suggestions for the project they make will begin to take on a haughty tone, and questions about their involvement in the leadership will regularly be provided (e.g., "I just wanted to help, but if I am not needed . . ."). This kind of person looks not to serve the vision but to find a way to benefit themselves or the things they lead.

We bring honor to those who have influenced and blessed us in the past by achieving the great goals and dreams that God has placed in our hearts, not by giving authority and prominence to people outside of their giftedness or capacity. Allowing a past benefactor access to the reigns of leadership in projects for which we are confident they will not succeed dishonors the project and those who invested in our transformational leader in the past. The contribution that they made in the past is real and worthy of appreciation, but not to the extent of giving a role for which they are ill suited or could even be harmful.

These are delicate and often touchy situations. When I encountered one while visiting a project, I deferred to the local leader to handle the situation and commented on my observations. Upon visiting the project again two years later, this meddlesome person appeared everywhere we went—from the bread store to a graduation ceremony—making promises and boasting in things he did have the capacity to fulfill, and thereby causing consternation among those present who knew better. After counsel, discussion, and regular repeats of the pattern by this person, I made an unusual invective to my partner: "If you want to work with this person who you agree does not have the capacity to perform the things he promises, that is your choice, but I must draw a boundary that he not be involved my activities, transport, etc."

The beauty of global leadership is that it all reduces to the same leadership issues that we all face, all around the globe. People are people, and we all struggle, strive, and fail. Eventually we get back up and try again, and if we are blessed to learn from our failures, we take a different course to avoid the shoals of destruction. Personal and corporate redemption are our worthy goals, but the individual timing will vary according to the individual, not by our design but according to their capacity and openness to the Holy Spirit.

10

Building the Vision Together

INSPIRATION AND COLLABORATION

The Process

LET US VISIT THE beach again and our sandcastles . . .

Sandcastles are inspired by our own engagement with the sand, to be moved and transformed by our bodies, and to be grown as well as we observe others building their castles. We watch as they dig moats and passageways to enter their compound, sections of wall and reservoirs for water from a bucket, or areas waiting to be filled by the next wave, or for the tide to do the work for them through channels specifically built for the work. As they fill with water, we jump for joy, and sometimes a little horror as the water starts to erode part of our creation. We quickly rebuild and fortify as we adapt our model to the realities around it.

Steps We Experience:

Idea	Chaos
Action	Complexity
Exposure	Counsel
Improvement	Order
Improvise	Enhancement

Organize/Structure	Stagnation
Repeat . . .	

The Challenge

There is a deadly tendency to have either *complete creativity* or *immovable management* control. Both are deadly on their own and equally deadly without each other. Inspiration and management are not in opposition; they just reside in different people and parts of the process that are equally necessary to complete the great things that God has for us. Jesus said, 'You will do even greater things than these . . .' (John 14:12, my paraphrase).

Inspiration and Exposure

Both managers and creatives need each other, and they need to be inspired together. But they are not expected to become each other. Rather they respect each other's gifts and use them in their appropriate places and seasons.

Inspiration

What if we never saw anyone else's sandcastle? What if we never saw a church or school other than the ones in our small village or farming community? What if we only saw schools in affluent suburbs or densely packed cities? In each case we would lack some of the necessary information to spur our creativity to the heights that God has in mind for the place we serve and the people we lead. We need heady, thorough exposure—without rushing into specific decisions and plans.

Stages of Dreaming and Vision

1. Everything is broken and needs to be repaired: *education, transportation, food, government.*

2. Pick one to start that you are most passionate about. *Education*! Great. What kind? Preschool, elementary, university? *All of them.* Great. Where will you start?

3. Define it. *Elementary education in a specific community.* You're on the right track.

4. Small dreams: Planners here are tempted to think up small dreams so as not to fail.

5. Expandable dreams: Planners think bigger about expanding in stages to achieve their true vision.

6. Multiplying dreams: Planners think and plan about expanding fruitfully over time by expanding the vision.

7. First phase implementation.

8. Second phase expansion of the original project.

9. Fruitful multiplication of the project and simultaneous expansion into other areas.

10. Mentoring new visionaries through their plans.

Trap of Small Dreams

Too many times, local leaders are trapped into small dreams based on perceived access to current, at-hand resources. Creatives can limit their dreams based on a lack of exposure to new ideas, and uncertainty and fear about future resources not materializing, due to observable experiences from the past. Managers also limit dreams based on a bias toward currently available resources and fear that the dreams will outstrip the finances. So, they have a tendency to believe new dreams should be tamped down, since the organization is now operating well, and their job is to keep things on an even keel, in an orderly way, all the time.

Miniaturized Version of Someone Else's Dream

Sometimes we are briefly wrested from our small dreams (a stifling reality brought about by limiting ourselves to what we already have or can see) when we go to a conference or seminar somewhere and view someone else's big dream—only to be foolishly enticed to return home to try to recreate and inflict someone else's dream on a people that are entirely unfamiliar with this dream. Or worse yet, we develop our "junior size" imitation of that other person's dream. The sort of hidden logic here—based on a scarcity mentality—is that "this must be the kind of dream that God blesses right now because my dream just isn't happening, so I need to reproduce this other person's dream the best way I know how so I can be a success . . ." Wrong!

Dreams, visions, and plans are meant to be intriguing, influential, and inspiring, not copied in some sort of cut-and-paste operation.

Exposure Inspires Creativity

In too many parts of the developing world, leaders have been deprived of the opportunity to *experience* other options for their communities. The other sad option is when someone from outside comes and inflicts ideas and ways on a group of people who function more as subjects in the process than actual participants or co-dreamers—let alone owners of the work.

THE STANDARDIZATION MYTH

In my early work partnering global leaders with those from the West, I thought we would be able to standardize a process and ministry model for our mission partners from around the world. This would make things efficient and workable, like a franchise; in this way we would have a storehouse of knowledge and a proven system that could be replicated. It fit perfectly with my business background and training. But it was not God's plan.

As we collaborated with these leaders, *we learned* that they had unique ideas, passions, callings, missions, and plans. It is a blessed and humbling experience to be connected to all the creativity that God has placed strategically all over the world, and God will send you those kinds of partners if you have the capacity to receive, encourage, and bless them.

Franchises Abound But Are Not the Norm

Yes, there is such a thing as Subway and McDonald's, even in places like Cairo and Paris, but these are the minority of establishments. Local food and customs dominate globally. Even though one can find international corporate brands all around the globe, one will also observe that a Wendy's cold ice cream in a cup is much thicker and colder in the United States than in Great Britain, where they do not share the U.S.'s obsession with ice-cold beverages. More importantly, there are far more non-franchise restaurants around the world than those of the franchise variety.

We must confess and repent of our obsession with control and specific, indelible forms of accountability, which at the root of our standardization models enslave people's initiative and potential, while stifling dreams and creativity. We are made in the image of the God who created the universe in all of its vastness and wonder. And he made this planet with all its fragile, beautiful, and intricate ecosystems and awesome interactions—from tiny flowers to blowing storms and erupting volcanoes. God makes people different as well, and he delights when they use the creativity given to them to make new things and to remake the broken things and places for the glory of God.

"... Behold, I am making all things new" (Revelation 21:5).

Indeed, we must be driven by values and practices that bring life, growth, and blessing as we follow the leading of the Holy Spirit. These will not always have a single, standardized set or format, but with a little creativity we can ensure that our systems of accountability are biased toward the blessing and release of creativity, and not the opposite. After all, every form of accountability is meant to serve the vision and not the other way around.

11

Mission Multiplication Through Strategic Investment

CORE VALUE: MISSION MULTIPLICATION

THE CENTRAL CALLING OF our mission is:

1. *Not* to focus on the unnecessary prolonging of necessary *relief* through aid,

2. But *to invest* in sustainable, locally led and controlled models,

3. To bring release to *every good potential in every person* in a community . . .

Our Model

This is achieved by investing in local entrepreneurial leaders' education and plans, so that the result of their work will be the multiplied blessing of God manifest in others, in tangible, practical, measurable, and positive ways demonstrating fruitfulness.

Definitions: Aid vs. Investment

- *Aid* is for the temporary protection of vulnerable persons in the wake of a disaster or a crisis.

- *Subsidy or transfer payments*: Long-term financial subsidies to the poor are not aid, as the duration exceeds the reasonable timeframe to restore order subsequent to a disaster, whether natural or manmade.

- *Investment* is the strategic insertion of capital to create medium-size businesses, jobs, and entrepreneurial opportunities, in turn to bring about economic diversification, agricultural innovation or expansion, and increased trade and market access.

Problems

- Problem 1: *Conflating* aid models into development goals and investment.

- Problem 2: *Prolonging disaster aid* and morphing it into development goals through subsidy payments, food donations, etc., which bring about a dependency cycle and decrease local capacity for growth and expansion.

- Problem 3: *Slippery Slope Trap.* Aid and workers arrive in the wake of a war or natural disaster with the goal of immediate comfort and restoration of order. However, once the aid arrives, it is determined that there was no order prior to the disaster in the first place and that great peril will result to the local population when the emergency aid is terminated. There is no plan. If there is no plan for a problem, we declare it a crisis and treat it with ongoing aid and subsidy payments, pending the plan's creation, creating a system of ongoing dependance, underachievement, and unsustainable sustainability outcomes. This is done to the harm and frustration of all.

Solutions

Instead, the solution lies in developing a comprehensive, locally designed and led strategy for investing in the economic expansion of the community, structured to target the things that will bring release from the problem(s) at hand and simultaneously promote thriving, wealth creation, and multiplication.

Consequences

If we do not plant resources that bear fruit, we will forever create deepening cycles of dependency, ever reliant on someone else's seed . . . and the one receiving will be deprived of not only the harvest and expansion but also the use of their gifts and wealth to bless them and others.

12

The Psychology of Dependance
(Giver and Recipient)

CONSTANT AID HAS MANY ill effects. It demoralizes creativity, distorts healthy and natural ambition, and breeds passive indolence in the receiver and false pride in the donor. Through continual aid we teach people to stand in lines with their hands out—*to run to the aid truck and line up with empty containers*—symbols of the emptiness that the donor organizations assume exist wherever they go.

PSYCHOLOGY OF EMPOWERMENT

Should we stop caring? Nowhere here is there the suggestion that nothing should be done to address the poorer parts of the world's challenges. Quite the opposite: We need to be deeply, personally, and vitally engaged in fostering the realization of transformational communities by building deep and long-lasting relationships of mutuality, relentlessly seeking solutions that bring that self-same recovery, revitalization, and expansive multiplication. This is not an unproven theory; it is happening quietly all over the globe.

Psychology of Donors

Donors who give from emotional appeal are not educated to look for multiplicative fruit from where they *invest* their giving and donations. Ultimately, they find themselves passive in their giving, having no better alternatives. This is not how businesspeople run their businesses, but it is how church leaders and charities have conditioned people to behave, not having the best solution among many but the one easiest to explain and fund.

After our heart strings are plucked by compassion and guilt, we are easy prey for fruitless schemes of moving food, cash, materials, and personnel around the globe. We continue pouring money into these enterprises relentlessly year after year, with no sign of real change in the underlying conditions—as if that was an acceptable outcome or how God intended it. But we must do *something*, we rationalize, "because we care."

After all, we are giving and showing compassion. That cannot be bad, can it? Or even better for the social justice crowd, we are taking wealth from the richer people and giving it to the poor to restore social justice.

The Curse

Yet, it is like having a child with enormous potential whom we keep dependent on us for all their needs—from food to clothing and cars and so on—for decades and decades, and somehow we consider ourselves caring and successful parents.

The Course

When children are young, they are called "dependents" because they are pendant on adults for everything. But we are raising them to be *independent adults*. They are dependent when they are born because they cannot walk, talk, or eat on their own. Over time they mature, receive an education, leave their father and mother, and take a spouse and start their own family (Genesis 5:31). This is the natural and normal process of life.

The Infantilizing Trap

The poor outcomes of long-term relief aid in the lives of the recipients lead one to believe that the benefits to the donor are greater than those to the recipients. The donors feel good knowing they are helping a poor child and have their guilt and shock assuaged. But they are denied the opportunity to engage their best gifts, abilities, and expertise with partners across the globe in transforming the underlying conditions that keep people poor and inhibit parents from providing for their children.

Join in the Blessing

In Amish communities there is a practice called "barn raising" where all the men in the community help their neighbor build a barn together. At the end they all have something to be proud of, and there is a long-term blessing to the family that received the barn as well as to the overall economic health and social expansion of the community. But without the work and investment to see real growth and change endure and expand and multiply, we end up missing the real potential of joy, and instead our donors get fatigued by so many requests that never end.

Avoid the Waste

Simplistic, orderly systems of transfer payments, relief aid, and food relocation require enormous logistical resources from freight trains and cargo ships to local truck and transport, creating vast inefficiencies while allowing and encouraging local resource capacity to deteriorate and dwindle. That is highlighted in the aforementioned book *When Helping Hurts* and is also explained in the illuminating 2014 documentary *Poverty, Inc.*

13

Problems
Money, Fraud, Abuse, and Control

Here are two problems that are competing for our attention: Number one is foreign design and control as a means of eliminating waste and corruption. Number two is local control without adequate financial controls to prevent abuses. Choose your set. . .

RAISING FUNDS THROUGH LOCAL BUSINESSES SOUNDS GOOD

"OK," one might say, "I see we need to grow economic systems. And the idea that a school, clinic, handicap service center, or senior home could be funded and run by the profit of local businesses dedicated to that purpose is intriguing. However, there are a lot of challenges and problems to overcome. Yes, of course, every path has its troubles, and there is no such thing as a trouble-free solution. But what about financial fraud and the mishandling of assets, how do we protect against that if we do not have control of the process and the money?"

Choose Your Set

Now we are getting at the truth. So, let's first choose the set of problems most likely to bring about the goals we have in mind.

Problems—we all have them. Just the kind and stage varies: birthing problems, child rearing problems, expansion problems, no growth problems, feeding problems, growing productivity problems, starving local resource problems, shrinking and declining problems.

If we set out to solve our problems, we will likely have some success in solving some of them, but we may be better off to consider *exchanging* our known set of problems for a different, more purposeful set of problems. Growth problems are highly preferable to problems of stagnation and decline.

Risk/Reward

"Sowing in tears. . . reaping in joy"—Psalm 125:5–6

In poor countries, the corn that one carefully places into the ground is both literally and figuratively taking the corn off the family table that could help them survive. If the planted corn does not germinate into a crop, the family will die that much sooner without the same corn that could have been eaten. So, one sows in tears, fearing the worst—no rain, too much rain and rot, lack of sun, rodents, bugs, weather that is too hot, weather that is too cold, on and on—all outside the farmer's control.

That is why on that day when the fields are full of a bumper crop that one labored for and worried about, the farmer reaps in joy!

All of life is a competition of choices with our resources and our environments. Get the crops in the ground before the rains come; we must beat the rain. Let the corn dry so it can be preserved. Get them harvested before the winter comes; we must beat the cold.

Competition from Our Very Conception

Always in a fight, one of the thousands of sperm made it to the egg first, and that is why you are you. To be planted in this world is dangerous. Women look for the man who will provide the best security for raising her offspring. Men learn skills of consistency, balance, and innovation to bring provision for their families.

Birthing Is Traumatic

Entering this world is no easy process for a newborn. It is a challenging and life-threatening process for both mother and child. The mother is screaming, and the baby comes out crying . . . But there is unbelievable joy after waiting for those nine long months. Then the real work begins of building a household of nurture, growth, love, and accountability, which honors God and is built on sacrificial love in the model of Jesus Christ.

Reaping in Joy!

If we want to make a substantial, life-altering difference in the world, it will require more than our $49 monthly donation to pay for a child on the other side of the world, and yet the rewards will be exponentially increased for both.

If we simply pay for a child to go to school and isolate our participation to the school without stimulating the local economic structures, where will this child work when they graduate? There will be no job for our grown sponsor child when they are done with school. This is already a huge problem in the developing world, and some countries are encouraging their best and brightest to emigrate to other countries to find jobs. That is a recipe for continued poverty and decline.

HANDLING MONEY: HEALTHY NECESSITIES, PROPER FINANCIAL CONTROLS

With that in mind, let us discuss the elephant in the room: *money.*

There are not multiple ways of keeping financial records. In other words, there is not a Western way of keeping records and an Eastern way, or a more rural way versus urban way. Over many years I have been told by my partners, "We don't keep records that way here." Quite simply the translation of that statement is "We're not keeping any records at all" or "Our record keeping is so loose that accountability is unlikely, and failure is almost certain."

Fatal Trap: "Just Trust Them . . ."

We've also heard things like this: "We value trusting in people and not offending them by forcing them to implement 'complex' foreign standards of keeping records, making regular bank deposits, and instituting robust financial controls. That will just not work here."

Our response: *garbage.*

Autonomy Breeds Efficiency and Accountability

One of the benefits of investing for growth and expansion in a local community without ongoing infusions of subsidized cash is that it forces the community project leaders to be self-auditing and accountable. If they fail, it is on them; no one is coming to bail them out. That kind of accountability is incredibly motivating and empowering. It gives them the opportunity to make new decisions in the face of difficulty that can reap great rewards relative to the risk.

14

Effective Standards

KEEP RECORDS

RECORDKEEPING AND FINANCIAL MANAGEMENT run across a spectrum of diligence and accountability, to looseness and inaccuracy with the potential of fraud and mismanagement. Good character is always desired, but poor or no recordkeeping is an enticement to financial mismanagement, now or in the future when our leader of good character retires. Inadequate financial controls based on trusting the character of specific individuals will eventually attract a disqualifying individual and destroy the reputation of everyone in the organization in the process.

In high-trust cultures (honor cultures), it is common for leaders to believe that their well-intended honor and trust earned over many years of faithful action will always result in well intended positive outcomes. This is simply not true.

The Trust System

A church preschool in Southern California had the same bookkeeper for over forty years. She handled the financial records of the preschool with absolute integrity and kept everyone well informed of the organization's financial status. The system worked well for a long time, so when she retired, they hired a new bookkeeper and retained the existing system based on trust, which had served them well all these decades.

The new bookkeeper was slow on reports and producing checks, and after a few years the preschool was bankrupt. However, she had been able to use the preschool's "trust in the bookkeeper" system to add a $50-thousand addition to her home, a new car, and had also taken $374,000 from the school and acquired debt for them for the first time without their knowledge.

Create Systems of Trust to Protect People and the Organization

We live in a world of complexity. We live with people who fail and are tempted by both simple and extraordinary challenges. And when people fail, when their character is tested, when difficulties come their way and monies are not handled with proper controls—there will be losses. Those losses will affect not only the person who mishandled the funds but the reputation and integrity of the ministry itself, and will limit future contributions, expansions, and so forth.

KEEP THE RECORDS UP TO DATE

Laxity in recording payments, accounting, bank deposits, untimely and inaccurate billing for services, late payment of bills, and reimbursements without written invoices are all practices that will bankrupt ministries and cripple them financially. Again, this is often justified by statements like "We like to trust people here," "We just don't do things that way here," "I just don't have time to go to the bank," "I keep the money in a box in my office—it's safe there," and "We trust each other here."

We Trust You to Do the Right Thing

We trust you as well! We trust that you will keep good records, that you will make timely deposits to the bank, that you will have multiple people count contributions and deposits and review the receipts, that you will deposit the money together (so that deposit amounts do not change in transit). We trust you completely to do all of these things, because we would not want any harm to come to this ministry or to the children and families it serves because we did not mutually act in a trustworthy, transparent manner with the resources that God has entrusted to us for his glory.

OUR CHARACTER IS REFLECTED IN HOW WE HANDLE RESOURCES

How we handle money is a sign of our personal and corporate organizational and ministry integrity. It denotes our work ethic and intrinsic character development. We are not trying to be preachy here; the reality is that the mishandling of funds or loosely handling funds—which is in fact the same thing—will wreak havoc on your ministry, diminish your partnerships, and ultimately bankrupt the good work that God has called you to do. It is not an area for compromise or laxity.

If someone is late for a meeting, we can give them grace. If they're late with a bank deposit, we can give them a warning. If it happens a second time, they have earned a reassignment, reprimand, or dismissal. This cannot be stated too emphatically. This goes all the way back to Jesus, as we know that Judas was the one tending to the money without proper controls and was seduced into delusions of his own authority and using funds for his own purposes (see John 12:6). This, as it turned out, corresponded to the fact that he was not as supportive of his leader as he could have been—with disastrous results.

This is not to say that all bookkeepers or people who are more laissez-faire about administrative matters are in fact people who will betray you. But I have seen this over and over in businesses, churches, and ministries all over the U.S. and around the globe. Even if they are not intentionally trying to undermine the leadership directly, their behavior may well betray and weaken the organization.

Questioning the Vision

A church in Indiana was experiencing continued growth and required a larger hall to host their events, so they hired an architect and came up with drawings and a budget. The bookkeeper and their spouse started to privately question the project to the pastor and then other leaders. The pastor and leaders addressed their concerns and answered their questions, but the doubting continued and eventually started spreading to the congregation. Finally, the bookkeeper resigned and left the church. In reviewing the church records, they found that the bookkeeper was not giving to the church.

Authority over money is a high-trust privilege that carries with it unspoken authority that can be extorted to other areas of influence at the discretion of the individual, even when such authority is not granted or officially requested. For those who handle the funds, their personal loyalty and integrity matter in the finances and well beyond to all other parts of the ministry or project.

Money Missing

I have received those desperate phone calls from all over the globe. "Pastor Jim, I have a problem . . ." As the money-missing story unfolds, and I ask questions about the systems and controls that were in place, I can hear the strain on the other end of the line as the panic washes over them for treating people so poorly as to not have adequate financial controls to protect them from harming themselves, their reputations, and that of the organization from what is now a full-blown crisis.

Final caution: If after these warnings you are still not convinced, I leave you in the hands of God.

BEST PRACTICES

1. All monies will be deposited in the bank at the earliest daily convenience (today).

2. No money shall be retained in the offices that is not secured in a locked space.

3. No money shall be kept in file cabinets, envelopes, folders, etc.

4. All persons receiving money for any purpose shall be informed of the policies related to handing money.

5. No money shall be kept with individual persons other than for the immediate purchase of equipment or necessary items.

6. Receipts will be obtained and turned in promptly for reimbursement

7. Only a small amount of petty cash shall be kept on hand if there is a locked and secure place to keep it on the premises.

8. A written receipt, preferably printed, shall be provided for all services and purchases.

9. Reimbursements shall not be made without written or printed receipts. (The only exception to this rule is when a receipt has been lost or misplaced. This shall be on an exceptional basis, and proof of purchase shall be provided. Any ongoing recurrence of loss of receipt or failure to produce any written receipt will result in no reimbursement, reassignment of purchasing responsibilities, or removal from the position, whether paid or volunteer.)

10. Persons wishing to use their own money for purchases for ministry or organization purposes shall provide an accounting of the expenditure(s) even if they are not requesting reimbursement.

Explanation on this final point: It is a great gift to have generous donors supplying various things for a ministry; however, everyone serves for a season, and when that season is ended, the ministry is expected to continue. Yet, it is difficult for that ministry to continue when others do not understand the nature and the amount of expenditure and the corresponding budget that the ministry has had in the past. The practice of an individual or individuals donating all of the items for that ministry without identifying the costs and expenditures to the leadership can have adverse results on the ministry and those who follow in the ministry, as they may be perceived to be expected to pay for items in the ministry that they may not be in a financial position to afford.

"I Just Pay for It Myself"

My friend Maja was fatally hit by a car while crossing the street carrying Christmas presents for poor children at a Christmas party in an impoverished neighborhood. She was the Sunday school director at her church for many years, and it had been her practice to make the purchases for the ministry out of her own resources as she saw fit. She also had utilized the budgeted amount from the church in the children's ministry and turned in receipts that were approved and reimbursed. However, the vast majority of the expenses were not reimbursed and were not turned in for payment; these undergirded the ministry for more than a decade.

After her tragic death, new leaders came to the children's ministry of the church, and they were profoundly unable to manage the ministry on the budget that the church had provided in the past. Their service and expenditure started to come into question: "Why are the expenditures so much higher now than in the past? What are they doing spending so much more money than was budgeted previously?"

Maja's memorial service was at 8 a.m., and the building was packed with standing room only, to give honor to her life of service and the Lord she loved. We do not want to unintentionally bring dishonor to those who will serve after us, and someone *will* serve after us, as we are all here temporarily.

To address this situation, the answer is manifestly clear from the facts stated above. So, we will do well to, at minimum, record *all* the expenditures accurately—those that are donated as well as those that are budgeted—so that we may well serve the organization now and into the future, in a faithful way that blesses those who have come before us and those who go after us.

FAITH WITNESS

Please, please, *please* hear this admonition: Be gracious and diligent as you deal with money. Understand and know that as you faithfully adhere to a policy, you are in fact treating people with the greatest kindness and respect that they will ever receive in their life. The system itself will prove that they are people of high trust, because it is a system of accountability, regularly verifying the trustworthiness of each person who operates within its policies, practices, and protocols.

What if they refuse to adhere and threaten to leave? Assure them they are loved and that our community policies are to protect and bless everyone. If they still refuse, let them go. People who make threats are dangerous. Listen to the rattle of the snake lest you are bitten. It may not be today or tomorrow, but a story will crop up in time that you will be grateful was lived out elsewhere and not with you.

We do not know if a person in progress who genuinely wants to serve has just stepped out the door, or a Judas may have stepped out to betray someone else and you are therefore blessed. Also, understand that the blame for lax financial practices related to money will at some point land on some unlikely or unsuspecting volunteer who is new on the scene; they will get blamed because they are new, and the assumption is that "things were fine" before they came on board. But when the matter is investigated, the fraud will usually go back for some time, and when the situation is finally resolved—even if they are found completely innocent—the mark of suspicion will linger over them unjustly for years to come. This is an unfortunate, unsettling, and unnecessary outcome.

"I Want My Treasure in Heaven"

The good-hearted reason that people give for not recording expenses or turning in receipts as a donation is often that they don't want credit or attention for their donation or generosity. Again, although this behavior is well intended, it places a future burden for those who come after us. We do not want to stifle generosity; therefore, a loving conversation that appreciates the donor's service is appropriate, while at the same time searching for solutions that will allow the ministry to continue without interruption. The donor could make a larger contribution to the organization's budget, but that does not mean the resources would be allocated to the ministry they have been funding. Thus, this is a way of increasing the budget without asking for permission from others and all that entails.

Note: Most people believe they are committed and have no intention of leaving the ministry they are investing in, but we are all temporary and have a responsibility for the present and the future after us. Legacy is the key factor here, for without a successor we are not a success. Creating a system that puts unnecessary burdens on those who follow us is not creating success.

Pride and emotions, self-worth and identity, as well as personal integrity, all get muddled together when we are dealing with or talking about money. It tends to be a highly sensitive subject. However, we must not allow the emotions or understandings that people have of themselves determine what our polices will be. We must determine to be faithful and accountable and conduct ourselves in ways that are above reproach today and tomorrow.

CONSISTENT POLICY

Consistent policy that is written down, published, and uniformly followed decreases some of these human proclivities and tendencies of taking personal offense for "financial controls" related to expectations for money, donations, and contributions.

"Don't You Trust Me? Please Make an Exception"

When we were building the first phase of a new building for a school in Cameroon, the rainy season was fast approaching, and our partner Andrew Jr. was desperate to finish the construction before the daily monsoonal rains came. Our policy regarding new construction was to release funds only after proof of completion for each phase of construction of the project was submitted and approved. This caused some delays, as moneys move slowly in international transactions.

Sample Reimbursement Schedule Policy:

- Purchase of property.
- Foundation completed—reimbursed.
- Block walls / electrical completed—reimbursed.
- Plumbing/well completed—reimbursed.
- Roof and truss framing completed—reimbursed.

Andrew pleaded with us to release all of the funds at once, so the project could move more swiftly and finish before the rainy season. We did not meet that request. Andrew asked me rather pointedly, "Don't you trust me? Can you not release all of the funds . . .?"

My response was, "We trust you, but we do not know how trustworthy all of the people who will come after you will be. We need to establish a system that applies to everyone that can be followed consistently, because if we have a major failure related to finances for a project, the projects may well lose the support of those investing in the projects, and the projects will end." I added, "This is God's project, and it is his responsibility to see it through—including the weather."

This turned out to be prophetic.

Unexpected Miracle

The project went forward, and the rainy season showed up as expected just after the foundation was poured. Each day the workers came to the building site and formed the concrete blocks on the site to be laid by the masons.

Each day it poured rain all around the area . . . except on the construction site. Each day while the workers were there, it rained heavily and created a muddy mess, but not on our construction site. On our site, it only rained at night when everything was covered with tarps. Those who watched the progress, including the government officials, all said the same thing: "Only God could do this."

Amen. To God be the glory! Trust God and give him the glory.

Trust

Money issues have an amazing way of showing God's power and providence. Money also reveals our own inner struggles and insecurities. We are building buildings, while God is building our faith.

Before the new building construction project began, our school was on a different piece of land, and as the school was rapidly growing, we needed more space. Andrew Jr. was attempting to buy a former chicken farm adjacent to the first school building site, and the deal had many ups and downs. When the seller realized there were partners in the United States, the price almost doubled over night.

Andrew Jr. was three weeks from finishing his master's degree and called me in a panic. He said he was going to leave school and board a plane immediately to return to Cameroon and get the deal for the buildings back on track. I asked Andrew to delay and have lunch with me. He was very agitated when I arrived; he was convinced that his new ministry and school were all about to fail.

Coaching

I told him, "Andrew, I do not have a solution for the purchase of the farm next door to the existing school building, but let's play a little game if you will indulge me." He was resistant, but ultimately went along, which is a testament to his commitment as a leader to his vision and the children the school is serving to this day.

I asked him, "How much would it cost to buy some land in the area where the school is?" We then explored how much land we would need, how much it would cost to erect the first three classrooms on the site, as well as installing a well and flush toilets with a septic system for the sewage. After we added all the numbers up, it came to less than the cost of purchasing and converting the smaller chicken farm. Further we ascertained that the old school classrooms could be converted into housing for the teachers and earn additional rental income, which would help with income for the school long term.

We left that lunch with a new vision for the ministry and an expanded goal for the school.

Obstructions May Be the Pathways to Bigger Dreams

Do not be surprised when money and project problems elicit emotions that may not seem appropriate to the occasion or the gravity of the problem. But also do not lose sight of the larger goal when calamities arise. Realize that many times when working in the majority world, the partners have not transacted these kinds of deals for land and buildings because of the poverty they come from. This brings added pressure not to fail. Also understand that every solution is not just a matter of money either; use creativity and look for the "yes," "no," and "have you considered?" possibilities that God is placing before you to expand the vision beyond what you might have imagined. It may just be miracle season.

FAITH IN ACTION

Our role is to support each other in these times. To prayerfully point each other to God and listen to the Holy Spirit. To think creatively and not get trapped into binary, "either-or" thinking (e.g., *Either* we get this property, *or* we fail and the whole mission will be lost"). This kind of thinking usually leads to poor decision making and poor outcomes. It requires faith to let one deal go and trust God for another that may not yet be in sight or at hand.

Change is disruptive and exciting. As we behold the new thing that God is doing, let us rejoice and give thanks at each phase and with each exuberant and halting step we make.

Prayer

"In everything give thanks . . ." (1 Thessalonians 5:18, NKJV).

Even as I write this section, I am sitting in a house purchased for International Theological Seminary, where I serve on the board. In nine months, we relocated the school, negotiated the deal for a new building, and purchased two others, while I sold my own house and was looking for the replacement (during Covid). None of those transactions went easily, and there are times when we think to ourselves, "We must make the deal work."

But we are not in control. Relax—it is in God's hands. Continue to go forward as you are able, trust in his provision, and prayerfully anticipate the unexpected blessings that will appear on the horizon, wrapped in the paper of trouble and challenges further perfecting his saints as they travail on this plain.

What was our unexpected blessing? This same year we began a new partnership with Yoido Full Gospel Church of Seoul, South Korea, to train their next generation of pastors serving outside Korea, around the world and in the U.S. God has a lot of surprises for you if you are willing to receive them.

15

Money and Mission Myths

MYTHS WORTH BUSTING

Myths of the Recipient, "Poor Class"

1. Others have money, and I am powerless without money.

2. I am inferior due to my lack of resources.

3. I must find someone with money to bless me (or I will always be helpless and poor).

4. Borrowing someone else's "money person" with my superior poverty plan is acceptable behavior, and this is likely my only chance to achieve independence from this poverty state.

5. Donors are smarter than recipients because they have more money.

Myths of the Wealthy, "Donor Class"

1. The developing world needs donations of our resources, as they are unable to care for themselves.

2. Our ways are superior because we have more wealth and therefore more knowledge.

3. Global poverty is mostly intractable, and finding good partners who will maximize my funding of the poor is the best we can expect.

4. We require financial accountability, but we are very busy and cannot be too involved.

5. The world needs our plan for church growth and proper teaching. We will "partner" with you in order to see our way copied all over the globe. You need us.

6. When poor people seek our help, it is because of our superior knowledge and ability. We are a commodity in demand and can behave as a high-value resource because we have wealth.

Myths of "Social Justice Warriors"

1. We are compelled as a matter of obligation to fight against poverty and for the oppressed in the name of social justice. Agreeing with this "value" is mandatory to make a difference.

2. Simply believing in *compassion* toward the poor is offensive and suggests an "optional" motif for the mandatory call to care for the poor and disadvantaged.

3. As social justice warriors, we are uniquely qualified to care for the poor and will commit to serving around the globe. Our passion and service qualify us as experts (no matter the outcomes). If we fail, there should be recriminations against those who did not follow us as well as legislation to force "our justice" on the economies and people of the world.

4. World governments from developed countries must move more and more money and resources to poorer, developing countries to achieve equity, as a matter of mandatory morality until poverty is wiped out. Some are poor because others have too much. We must reduce the wealth of the rich in order to lift up the poor. Failure to act in agreement means you oppose the cause of justice and are therefore a selfish contributor to global poverty and suffering.

5. We have the most in common with the poor because of our stance on the mandatory nature of enforcing social justice through governmental intervention and the value of mandatory movement of monies from wealthy nations, even though we do not actually have personal, listening relationships with the poor.

DREAMS WORTH DREAMING

Dreams of the Developing World

1. We dream of finding a true partner to work with long term in a mutual relationship, to see a community transformed from poverty.

2. We long to be respected and listened to as a fully informed, local expert on the community we serve.

3. We want to be trusted to build a local leadership team to lead and implement change on a local level, with autonomy to produce results without extraneous outside mandates.

Dreams of the Wealthy, Donor Class

1. Our dream is to participate with a community that is effectively moving out of poverty by strategic investment to sustained and growing advancement.

2. There must be a better model for fighting poverty than constant and regular donations with no real economic growth. Why is it not possible to grow poor communities through strategic business investment to create sustainable, expanding economic growth?

3. What are the new and innovative approaches being made to see poverty systems transformed bringing about wealth creation and the betterment of the people in the community?

4. How can we address poverty without getting caught up in the graft of corrupt government systems?

Dreams of Social Justice Warriors

1. We yearn to see the global poor empowered to live up to their potential with food security, fair wages, education, and access to medical care.

2. Our dream is to see just governments that protect their citizens and fight against injustice and oppression.

God is watching. He is giving us invaluable opportunities in this era to connect around the world in real time and make a real impact in ways never before possible. At the same time, we are reminded that we will be rewarded for how we treated "the least of these," those who could not pay us back or be used to help us get ahead.

"Then the righteous will answer him, saying, 'Lord, when did we see you hungry and feed you, or thirsty and give you drink? And when did we see you a stranger and welcome you, or naked and clothe you? And when did we see you sick or in prison and visit you?' And the King will answer them, 'Truly, I say to you, as you did it to one of the least of these my brothers, you did it to me'" (Matthew 25:37–40).

16

Compassionate, Relational Social Justice

"JUSTICE" IS, UNDERSTANDABLY, THE captivating motivation for many readers here, and the model proposed should be expanding the view that justice can be impactful in practical actions and positive engagement with leaders studying in the developed world from the majority world. The resulting consequences—of working together to actually transform a community through job and education opportunities, to truly care for those who are struggling by empowering them economically—will be *the blessing that the poor actually seek.* This takes the place of just loudly protesting for those we do not yet personally know, and even appear to personally ignore.

However, the opportunity is now available for our personal involvement in connecting leaders of the local poor with businesspeople who have the skills to bring about true, sustainable economic justice through empowerment of local leaders and the communities they serve. Dive in—the water is fine.

LEARN FROM WHAT HAS NOT WORKED

It is time to expand to workable solutions beyond various-sized subsidy payments and donations, which are passionately advocated for but nevertheless perpetuate the extreme poverty they intend to fight. Another long-term solution strategy that begs to be sidestepped is the exclusive pursuit of influencing governmental agencies through intergovernmental cooperation, which takes years and is subject to enormous corruption, fraud, and ineffectiveness.

Be Inspired to Try New Ways

Do you know which business models work right now? They are the ones led and designed by local leaders to address local problems through local ownership and indigenous expansion of the local economy through transformational practices. This is a place where a real and immediate effect is made, based on building relationships and supporting those leaders while they study in the United States. The challenge for the social justice crowd will be listening to these global leaders as their horizons are spread and they discover new options and opportunities to employ systematically while they are here.

Things You Will Learn

These leaders have their own way of thinking, and the vast majority already appreciate the United States and like the country before they come, and even more so after living here. The vast majority will privately say that they cannot understand how anyone can say this is the worst country in the world. The African students do not relate to BLM ("Black Lives Matter") as a movement, and they were unimpressed with Barack Obama as a leader. All of their leaders are black, so his ethnicity was nothing special to them when it comes to analyzing and observing a leader's effectiveness.

Social justice warriors will struggle in not forcing their agendas on students studying here to return home and bring transformation. You are encouraged to do more listening than speaking. Visit their country and community to come to a clearer understanding of the circumstances they are working with, and to see the faces of the real people so often spoken of but never met face to face. Bless them through praying with them; let them lead. Eat with them; eat their food. Listen to them and serve them before putting forth your social justice beliefs. It can take one to two years for them to honestly share their beliefs about sensitive topics, particularly because other people tend to assume their thoughts and convictions based on their skin color and place of origin, which is a foolish if not racist act.

PRACTICE PRACTICAL SOCIAL JUSTICE

What specific issues can governments be influenced to change in order to reduce poverty conditions? The worst policies that play a key role in exacerbating poverty are as follows:

1. Lack of access to markets, foreign and domestic.
2. Access to purchase and hold a clear title to land.
3. A legal system that protects individual property-ownership rights.

Land

One of the top reasons many people cannot thrive is the lack of ability to own land with a clear title. Much work is needed to reform the socialistic government land practices that perpetuate modern-day serfdom globally. Corruption through government and favored business relationships, nepotism, and crony business relationships lock the poor out of economic potential to only benefit high-ranking government officials and oligarchs. We must work for land rights and employment rights that do not end with feudalistic certainty upon the election of a new president.

Infrastructure: Roads, Bridges, Communication, Water, Electricity

Our marching orders are to strive for infrastructure reform, another key to economic growth and empowerment. We must work for the removal of cartels and organized crime that is sucking the life out of poor countries. We do this by facilitating the opportunities of people having the tools to create wealth from their own hands. These are literal tools with which they can work and earn a living: saws, hammers, sewing machines, stylist chairs, commercial cooking pans and ovens, etc. With these tools in place, the governments are less likely to interpose themselves to disenfranchise through corruption.

That is the "social justice need" of the hour. Work on processes, programs, and accountability that bring about free speech and property rights reforms—that is where the difference will be made.

CAREFUL EXAMINATION

Examine not just the motives of others but your own as well. Choose intentionally. Choose to learn from past behavior and not be mired in red-hot inflammatory rhetoric alone. Choose from the areas of effectiveness that we have been describing. Care for the poor individually—as people you know personally—as an act of love, engagement, and ongoing listening through relationship with them.

Avoid

Avoid the virtue signaling of hanging out with those who say they care for the poor and swap slogans, talk protests, share pamphlets, insult and shout down opponents, as they obstruct through sit-ins and activism "for the poor" but where there has not been relationship by being with and among the poor of the world. This means showing you care for the poor by being in their village or community, listening to and learning from them, loving them, knowing their names, learning about their communities and their strengths and celebrations. This is not like the virtue signalers who just post on social media *#CareForThePoor* but have never visited, lived, or even slept overnight in a poor community.

Here are other things to staunchly avoid:

- Caring for the poor as a point of personal pride—narcissism— without actual love for the poor themselves as real flesh-and-blood people, who want to know someone who cares enough that they visited them.

- Caring for the poor as a means to assuage personal or corporate guilt. What the world needs is love and friendship, not a formula of intersectional victimhood rankings. Certainly, the poor have no desire to keep defining their oppression; they just want a way out as soon as possible.

- Care for the poor as an act of unintentional hospitality. They are here in your country studying to change the world; invite them into your home and your church. Build ties and have your universe expanded. Avoid the easy temptation to hate your country when others admire it and have even come here to learn and take home its better aspects.

- Going on trips to places where you will never return or eventually lose interest. The majority world and the global community make lifelong friendships, not relationships of convenience.

BE PREPARED

Be prepared to have your own privilege challenged in new ways that you did not anticipate; otherwise you are wasting the opportunity being placed before you. Learn from those who are studying here on American soil—what they admire about your country and what surprises them—and be willing to listen and have your assumptions and beliefs upended about their questions, hopes, and dreams. They may have very different ideas about social justice than you do; they are in the position to help you understand genuine poverty, suffering, and oppression like you have never experienced.

Dream big. Start small. Make measurable progress.

Essential Element IV

Project and Organization Leadership

*Adapting for Completion and Types
of Leadership Roles on the Team*

17

Overcoming Obstacles to Complete Projects

FINISHING THE TASK

THE IDEA OF DOING great things is infectious. *Creating dynamic transformative change* is a great dream and very motivating. However, getting trapped in bureaucratic cycles and watching your dreams wither amidst red tape and endlessly overlapping requirements, schedules, and necessary sequencing can ultimately kill a project before it even gets off the ground. Achieving goals requires overcoming inevitable obstacles that block and destroy project completion.

Empowering communities is not a democratic process where everyone is given an equal share. Change bubbles up from the ground. Change happens through empowering goal seekers! Established, proven leaders have the ability to mobilize others to action, while identifying specific challenges and problems, overcoming them, and seeing the project through to fruition. (Be wary of idealized dreamers who cannot lead themselves out of bed in the morning.)

"But we want to help everyone and give everyone a chance!" Good, that will be achieved by empowering leaders who can build things big enough to bless the most people, not by giving equal handouts. Equal handouts will not build a school building, or a clinic, or any other project.

Goals are great; completion is better.

WORKING HARD

Hard work is not enough to finish a project. Inevitable obstacles will arise that are in direct proportion to the size of the project. Evil will find subtle and invasive ways of undermining any project of significance. Plan for it; do not be surprised by it. Those who are hard workers will instinctively believe that they need to work harder or stay at the project longer hours, but that alone will not overcome obstacles. They are just beating their head against the obstacles harder than before, hoping for a different outcome that is not in the offing.

New Directions

Moving a rusted bolt lose with a wrench is quite difficult, but one of the most effective and nonintuitive ways to loosen a rusted bolt is to tighten it first. Once the bolt is loosened in any direction, it is loosened for any direction, including removal. Doing the job is not the same as achieving the goal. Showing up on time with your wrench and going through the motions—making the right calls and contacts in fulfilling the job description—is not the same as goal achievement.

"It Can't Be Done"

That phrase is one of the biggest motivators in my life. When I am told something cannot be done, a wry smile will creep across my face, and it is like, *Challenge on!* From there we slice and dice every project component, every participant and point of sequencing to determine potential alternate pathways to achieve our goals and bring about actual solutions for resolution.

ILLUSTRATION

Goal: Gain Approvals for Increase Preschool Enrollment

When the preschool at a church where I was the pastor grew from fifty to over one hundred students, we were required to update our license with the state government. They gave us a whole list of things that would be required: updating the classrooms, adding a sink, updating smoke alarms, expanding the fenced play area for the children, and more.

Delegated Authority

The project was under the authority of the preschool director, the associate pastor, and supported by the church administrator.

Approvals Required

They had to get approval from: the city building department, the city fire department, and the state board that oversaw preschools. The project was to take three months, but nine months later the reports that came to me were the same: "We are working on it."

Necessary Steps:

1. Add outdoor play area.
2. Modify fencing for play area.
3. Remodel classroom.
4. Relocate supply room.
5. Get the necessary permit from the state government, with inspections and approvals.
6. Get approval from the city fire marshal, building department, and the state preschool inspector.

Check-ins

"How is it going?" I asked at our weekly leadership team meeting. All was in progress, they told me, as the proper procedures and sequencing had been identified, and the process was being worked and would come to completion. Good.

Nine months later. . . "We are still working on it!"

Analysis

As a leader, I failed them. Everyone was calling the appropriate persons and entities, but they were not getting results, and every delay pushed the project further and further out.

Every change in a project is a potential and actual delay to the completion date. Even if the change is an enhancement to the project—bringing higher value, utility, and scalability—it still has an immediate cost. These delays cost us $90,000 that was not budgeted.

Cause: Frustration with the Permitting Process

Frustration is not getting a call answered or returned. It is finding out that people quit who had been part of the approval process and having to start all over again with someone new. Everyone was frustrated and felt like a victim. None of them wanted to disappoint me or the elders, so they tried their best alone, with their own resources, plugging away at the goal with the same methods, and failed. Frustration is just the devil in disguise.

Overcome Frustration with Persistence and Creative Problem Solving

Frustration is not just a call to persistence; it is a call to tenacious and hyper-creative problem solving, prayer, and passionate redirection of actions that bring results! Frustration is a call to creativity—to dynamic, dysmorphic engagements with change factors as malleable ingredients, or lynch pins, or dominoes. What is the one thing we could change that would move this whole situation that we have not yet considered?

Skilled identifiers of key change components have the ability to bring great change at great speed. Persistence in identifying, maneuvering, and manipulating the right components into their new change position is key.

Great surgeons have the skill of manipulating the organs, ligaments, and tissues they are working on in a sequential symphony of relationship that allows death-defying restoration. Along the way there are inevitable obstacles that require necessary adjustments, as well as compensations for weak points and limitations that the new solution is creating, which, if ignored, can cause catastrophic failure. These must be addressed with relentless attention, precise movement, and extraordinary skill.

PRODUCTIVE REALIGNMENT

We cannot wish obstacles away or wait for a better outcome in the future. This is the moment for action.

When a successful modification step is achieved, everyone breathes a sigh of relief anticipating movement toward the next step. We wipe the sweat from our brows. We take a glance at the team, make eye contact, and let each other know that together we did it, and now we can go on and finish the task.

Key Component

For the above preschool project, it was the microwave in the kitchen that caused the turmoil. The fire chief had not previously noticed the microwave oven in the kitchen, but on final inspection, his verdict was that the building required a smoke detector immediately above the microwave. This set the multistage, government-approval process and contractor-sequencing fiasco back into full swing. It was a tangled web of contingencies, schedule conflicts, and bureaucracy.

I won't bore you with the details any further, but there was a simple solution: *remove the microwave.* The microwave could be removed, and the school could function using one of the other kitchens on the campus until a smoke detector was installed prior to the microwave being returned. (For the record, if you recognized this solution, you have consulting skills that others need.)

Change efforts often fail because the difficult tasks are avoided, ignored, or remain invisible because we cannot see past the stalled step, which we are repeatedly addressing in the same fashion, over and over, without results. A skilled practitioner anticipates the obstacles. The more they have persevered through these kinds of challenges, the more they anticipate potential obstacles and prepare plans and timelines to account for them, anticipated as well as unanticipated. When we have a plan for the anticipated and unanticipated, and when we are ready to think creatively and adaptively to the situation, we are not stuck or surprised for long. But how can we have a plan for what we do not anticipate?

Planning for the Unplanned

First, give the anticipated/unanticipated a column on the spreadsheet and on the calendared timeline. That way, when these elements appear, you already have a space for them. In construction the term used is "general conditions," meaning what is happening on the construction site that was unseen before the project began.

Completing the renovation of an existing building is more expensive than new construction from the ground up. The reason is the unforeseen expenses incurred when opening up an old structure and rectifying them. This inevitably brings frustration, delays, emotional upheavals, and unwanted surprises that most people are not welcome to experiencing. Likewise, without the proper expertise, knowledge, and connections, one can easily be taken advantage of in the costs—implementing the right options required to take care of the unanticipated challenges and their relative costs. Different people will give different information. Because of these hassles and expenses, people opt out of managing large disruptive projects in their homes and pay more for a new home or one that has already been remodeled, simply because they are too disruptive and unpredictable. It is also why a good profit can be made by a good builder remodeling and selling homes. Similarly, a big loss can ensue from hiring a good builder and ignoring their advice, hoping to save a few dollars only to later spend thousands.

Bad or Incomplete Information

A city official told an acquaintance of mine that she could not remove a large tree from the backyard of a home where she planned to build an addition. However, the official only told her part of the information. The city municipal code actually stated that if the tree was removed, another similar tree must be planted to replace it, one for one. That is a different scenario altogether, and it gives alternate options that were not presented in the first statement (which was true but only partially so).

Minimize Mess Through Proper Sequencing

As an example, a good builder knows when to paint in the process of construction. Painting should be done after most of the messy work is complete. But it should be done before the installation of cabinets and flooring, especially carpet. Why? You want an even, clean job where the painter is not working up against surfaces that disturb their work or that can be damaged in the event of a spill or simple overspray.

Building is, by nature, a messy business, so the question is how to keep the mess from messing up the project.

Refuse the Mess

I know a pastor who, upon being hired at a church, told the leadership that he would conduct no building or remodeling projects at the church. He was convinced that they were messy, time consuming, and ultimately frustrating. This pastor was right; such projects are in fact hard, messy, and distracting work, but sometimes they are necessary for the mission.

Project completion, cost certainty, conflicting systems, organizational structures, decision making, and the comfort that people require to make it through significant changes together—all of these conspire against disruptive change, creativity, and new initiatives. New initiatives bring both tension and joy. They involve processes of uncertainty that cannot be anticipated and require judicious handling to achieve the specified goals.

18

Creative Change Agents

DETERMINING THE NATURE OF CREATIVE CHANGE AGENTS

CREATIVE CHANGE AGENTS ARE acute problem solvers. They don't just think outside the box—they have never been inside the box and have little interest of ever entering. They enjoy the challenge of creating and inventing new things, looking for solutions in unlikely places. They are well versed in many areas and borrow freely from different disciplines to create unique, innovative solutions to new or existing realities.

Not All Problems and Solvers Are the Same

A friend of mine sees the same solution to most problems. She has done "some" research on many things and has great confidence as she applies the same solution over and over—whether or not it fits. She is confident and assured in her method and looks for the preferred signs and symptoms to which she can apply her approved method as the proposed solution for every problem. With this method, new symptoms are ignored or denied as to their veracity; it is only necessary to find the symptoms that point to the solution that she has at hand. Quick with advice yet regularly overwhelmed by her own problems that she cannot overcome, my friend is in a quandary likely because she seeks the selfsame solutions over and over. If one has a big hammer, it is easy to see everything as a nail.

As leaders, teachers, and preachers, many of us give the same solutions over and over, without regard to the complexity and nuance of the underlying facts of a given situation. We breeze past any pesky facts that do not align with our preferred solution or diagnosis model, which in fact become one in the same over time and can perpetuate as much harm as they do good.

Life is a cornucopia of learning and revelations from others that regularly enhance our effectiveness in dealing with situations. They lend us the ability to deduce causes and factors that go beyond our prejudices and tropes; thus, we delve into deeper understandings of the causal structures and tentacles of problems that entangle so much of the positive, productive, and transformational change that we desire.

PERFORM A CUSTOMIZED PROBLEM HISTORY

If you want to be a creative change agent, here is my advice.

Deduce the facts. Look for mitigators and outliers that may not have been anticipated. Align each symptom with an explainable and causal source. Do not lazily ignore the things that do not fit your current paradigm of diagnosis or treatment. These are new opportunities in the school of life to learn and grow in effectiveness and compassion.

Medical professionals are taught how to do a medical history as part of their training. This can provide clues as to what potential causes could be instigating the current symptoms. When arriving at a doctor's office, one receives a medical questionnaire, especially when seeing a new doctor or specialist. The questionnaire enables them to direct their questions and inquiries more accurately, to find causes and cures.

Family History

When addressing most relationship problems, research beyond the couple's or individual's current crises is essential. The only common thing about problems is that they occur; beyond that, they have their own idiosyncrasies, which require due diligence in unearthing and identifying before a complete cure can be identified.

Again, there is a tendency in dealing with problems to adhere to a certain diagnostic syncretism, where all problems and solutions collude in such a way that we are accustomed to in our specialty, while we ignore some potential unseen causes to our own peril or the potential harm of others.

"She Needs a Counselor. . ."

That was the diagnosis from a board-certified neurologist from a prestigious pediatric neurological group in Pasadena, California, for my eleven-year-old daughter when she had stopped speaking to us, after previously displaying symptoms of memory loss. The medical history that the doctor took was wildly truncated from the other medical histories that we had participated in, from the other twenty-plus doctors we had seen looking for a diagnosis for my daughter's strange symptoms and behavior. "*She needs a counselor. . .*"

In the next ten days, my daughter experienced two subsequent grand mal seizures that were witnessed. It turns out that she was having nightly seizures and threatening hallucinations in her sleep, but we were unaware until one of her seizures was observed by a church youth leader during a youth retreat. This leader who witnessed the seizure had seen them before in a sibling afflicted with a seizure disorder.

Confirmation Bias

At the doctor's office where the counseling was suggested, my daughter was the only child in the waiting room not wearing a football helmet. That may sound like a strange observation, but this medical practice had a preponderance of children with severe seizure disorders that regularly threw them to the ground; they were subject to potential severe head trauma that would likely exacerbate their condition and cause additional injuries, so they wore helmets to protect themselves.

In contrast, my daughter, although subdued and withdrawn, could answer questions (reluctantly when compared to her former, exuberant self). She could walk into the office unassisted and sit on the examination table, and she never had had a seizure that we knew of. The doctor who did this very cursory ("grade D") medical history started telling us about how her own teenage child did not talk to her very much anymore, another conflation of life and experience of her own without searching out the facts for my daughter.

This laxity of approach in searching for facts that might shed more light on the underlying problem, if prolonged, could have potentially caused my daughter's death. It certainly led to more brain damage, as all of her childhood memories were wiped out by the eating away of her brain from lupus SLE, an autoimmune disease where the body's white blood cells consume healthy parts of the body misidentified as an infectious, invading disease. The body literally kills itself.

An entire book could be written about this experience, but Megan experienced fervent prayer by hundreds of people locally and from our global partners, and God performed many miracles that confounded her diagnosed outcome of brain damage and poor life performance. She returned to school after hospitalization within two weeks, not three years. Her speech was restored, she graduated salutatorian from high school, and most recently she completed her doctorate in occupational therapy from USC. To God be the glory.

LOOK FOR A UNIQUE FACTOR YOU HAVE NOT SEEN BEFORE

Please, whether you are a seasoned problem solver and analyzer of situations to bring change, make it a rule to look for potentially unique factors that you may not have encountered before. All the familiar signs may be there, and you may well be ready to spring into action with your planned solution, but take the time to listen and ask well, so that nothing important is missed. Find their "unique factor." It will flesh out what you already know and give you more nuanced insight into triaging solutions in the future.

For people who are highly intuitive, this can be an even more difficult practice. When the solutions to situations present themselves to you before most people are even aware there is a problem, it can seem pedantically slow and unnecessary to engage in what appears to be a fruitless search for additional information when the solution manifestly appears to be at hand and potential delay could be harmful.

Look for the New Facts Along the Way

It is possible to run in the speed and authority of intuition while keeping an eye open for new and additional facts. Even the best of experts can be wrong.

When my daughter was finally hospitalized at Children's Hospital Los Angeles, the head of neurology eventually became her primary physician. This doctor and his whole team were looking for answers to why this little girl was going silent. A PET scan was planned and run; numerous blood tests and a spinal tap were performed. Neurological aspects were initially explored by the head of the pediatric neurology department and multiple interns before care was shifted to rheumatology.

Do Not Reject the Facts That You Do Not Like

On the morning of the second day at the hospital, Dr. Peter Lim phoned in the results of the blood work that he had performed to the neurological medical team at the hospital from his office. The medical interns then relayed it to the head of neurology, who proceeded to berate them and dress them down in public for giving her the "wrong data." My daughter's white blood cell count was so extremely high (one of the signs of active lupus SLE) that the head of neurology was convinced the interns had gotten it wrong, wasting her time.

Inventing Our Own Reality

Sometimes as leaders in Christian organizations, we overlook flaws in potential team members, as we prefer to see the best side of people and their potential. So, when we come across information that is not flattering to an individual, we want to ignore it and instead work to "help them." We desire to see grace manifest in someone's life.

However, accepting people as they are with their real weaknesses and struggles is a better place to begin than giving them authority in an organization based on an imagined future where we hope they will be in a time to come. Hope for the future is good. Unfortunately, much harm can come in the present when people are not properly vetted, equipped, and prepared for the roles assigned to them.

There are times when addressing a problem with our solution (or relentlessly searching the inadequate ghetto of our limited solutions of current expertise), we cannot accept what seems incongruous to our theories and values.

Back at the hospital, the head of neurology finally demanded to see the results from the blood work and subsequently retreated from her attack without apologizing to the interns (a professional privilege in the field, apparently). She then pursued a new track with the rheumatology department, which quickly took over the case.

We must accept the full set of apparently conflicting pieces of data in a problem in order to pursue a complete, solutional picture for the problem. This will allow the creation of a more wholistic approach that can address the true totality of underlying causes.

19

Managing Resources Faithfully

MANAGERS AND VISIONARIES

VISIONARY CREATIVES ARE THE people who are often entrepreneurs. They create and have many ideas, but administration is not their forte, and they lose interest in running the day-to-day of an organization. This is why every great innovator needs a manager.

Identifying Managers

A good manager serves the interests of the owner and takes a strong participatory interest in the predictable outcomes sought, through reliable systems and practices, to maximize profit and the satisfaction of the customer being served. A bad manager consumes or wastes the resources of the owner to serve themselves and their own interests, while limiting innovation as an unnecessary and unpredictable cost.

Put Your Hand to the Task: "Watch with Your Eyes"

I was helping my friend Bamu repair several heaters that were not functioning at the seminary. The chaos that brought us to this point is not relevant here, but suffice it to say that after eight months, two managers, and three leadership teams, the task was not accomplished—and everyone was still cold.

In the process of replacing a thermostat that had gone missing, Bamu and I were both holding the new thermostat as we were installing it (in less-than-ideal conditions in this old building). Each of us held the thermostat and maneuvered it in the direction we saw fit in which to mount the new thermostat, which meant nothing was lining up. I realized that two managers were contending to use their leadership gifts at the same time. So, a test was in order.

"Bamu, let me hold the thermostat and you watch," I said.

"Yes," he verbally agreed, but his hand remained on the thermostat.

Seeing that I could not properly align the thermostat on this broken concrete wall with both of us holding it, I replied, "Bamu, I thought we agreed you would watch."

"I am. . ."

"Bamu, I need you to watch with your eyes and not with your hand."

We both laughed. Then it occurred to me: I have a new manager for my crew.

Definition: Manager of People

A good manager takes the task seriously, is committed to its completion, and has the ability to see the task through by resourcing the active, productive, and positive involvement of others, leveraging their ability in a multiplicative way to achieve the goal and advance the team's unity and collective skills.

TRUST WITHOUT VERIFICATION

Bako gave responsibility for managing a "micro," a small bus, to a man to earn income for the ministry that owned the micro. The man who recently had stopped using drugs as a result of the ministry dutifully drove people and charged for the service, keeping the mini-bus active at all times. There was a lot of activity, but no income came to the ministry whatsoever.

When the micro was needed by the ministry, the driver said he would drive it for them. Bako wisely deferred and indicated that he already had another driver for the occasion. The first driver was insistent

on being available to drive, but Bako calmly declined, reiterating that another driver was already secured. When it came to retrieving the micro, it
was with great difficulty and some persistence that they were finally able
to acquire the ministry's bus from the driver.

First Payment: Asset Loss

Upon inspection, the micro was missing parts. It no longer had a spare
tire or jack, and the tool kit was also missing along with the radio. There
were many stories to accompany the missing items, but Bako decided
that the time for stories would need to be continued on another occasion.
Wisely, the driver did not receive an opportunity to drive again.

When we waste grace, we are inserting ourselves in the place of
being the Savior. This is dangerous ground to stand on, and as we allow unfaithful servants to control, utilize for personal gain, and devalue
items for a ministry, we become their accomplices, no matter how well
intended our hopes may be at the beginning.

Second Payment: Reputation

Our costs will not end there either. An unfaithful manager or employee
will not shrink away when a legitimate failure has occurred. No, they
will blame you for causing them hardship by taking away their livelihood; they will claim that you are insensitive and gave them no warning
of termination. Of course, in the case of the micro, any earlier warning
would have resulted in the vehicle also missing its wheels or engine, and
stripped of its seats, by an "unknown thief."

Third Payment: Organizational Debasement

A bad asset manager can quickly become a thief, and if not corrected and
realigned, he or she will be subject to removal. Failure to remove them
will then inspire those they work with to follow their pattern of faith-
lessness. When we empower or leave in power those who are unfaithful
(despite good intentions), we are in fact empowering their values in our
organizations. The very values that they are exercising are well noticed by
those who work with them, and they will believe those to be the actual

values of the organization in practice, despite what is printed, promoted, or pontificated.

Fourth Payment: Donor Loss

The impulse toward using the business assets of the ministry for restoration instead of producing income will harm the ministry, and this leads to a loss of donor trust and support. No matter if the decision is well intended, the poor use of assets, human resources, and organizational reputation demonstrate the leader to be unable to coordinate the use of resources. Thus, they will quickly find themselves facing the fate of the unfaithful manager (see Luke 16)—removal from authority over said assets.

Fifth Payment: Organizational Retribution

As alluded to above, anticipate and expect the unfaithful manager to attack the leader who is finally holding them accountable. They will also naturally seek retribution against those who work under them or are indebted to them in any way. The driver may well accuse the person to whom he sold the spare tire and jack of theft and place them in jeopardy, in order to extricate and cover over his damaged reputation.

It Is Not Done Yet—More Damage Is on the Way

We wrongly assume that the bad manager, once confronted, will return to a healthy moral conscience, and that an accompanying positive practice will ensue from our corrective actions. But the character flaws are deep here and must not be minimized—nor broadcast against them to bring shame in order to restore our healthy reputation and role either.

Despite the fact that the bad manager is displaying his or her true character, in time they will play the victim and speak of the financial difficulties that pressed upon them, saying that any reasonable person would have given them more warning and grace in such "tough times." The thief now becomes the victim, and the person bringing correction becomes a heartless attacker of the weak.

No Grace for You!

At this point, the well-intended, faithful leader is desperate for approval for correcting the past errors and finally making the tough decision that was due long ago. But in fact, the leader who put this asset manager in place—whether by their own action or the benign acceptance of their predecessor—and yet failed to receive proper income and care of the asset has empowered and blessed this behavior, showing indifference to the overall ministry by this "benign neglect." No thanks are coming; the action is long overdue and will not be rewarded.

Even if a leader chose to squander their own resources, under their personal discretion, it will still affect their reputation (and as such is a disqualifying event for maintaining a leadership position). But when it enters the ministry or business the leader is responsible for, they bear the responsibility as well. This responsibility only grows and increases as time is added to the equation, creating a multiplying effect on the poor decisions of the past.

Sixth Payment: The Lost Ones

Finally, consider the faithful servants who could have held this position and longed to bless the ministry or supporting business through their faithful service, but these instead were passed up in favor of the unfaithful servant (the perpetual victim). In contrast, the ignored faithful ones take their request to God and ask, "How? Why?" And as they weep, the heart of God is moved against this injustice, which the leader is right in the middle of because he or she has in fact been playing God.

Without taking responsibility, the unfaithful servants remain in their blame state, never achieving, ever betraying, and ever blaming the world, friends, leaders, and even God. They have not hit their low point yet, which would open them up to change.

DESIRED OUTCOME: CHANGED LIVES

Character and behavior change positively when the weight of our own indiscretions is placed on our own heads. Only when the cost and pain of our behaviors rest directly with us do we change to delimit the personal discomfort of the consequences of our behavior. Only through the conviction of wrongdoing where the weight completely rests on one's own head can a person be moved to repent, confess, and seek forgiveness and a new start through restoration, acknowledging the harm they have caused and repaying those they have harmed. Those with an unrenewed conscience, or an impaired conscience that is being restored, are not moved by the pain that they cause others. They simply seek new opportunities to practice the lifestyle and pattern that they have established through the intricacies of their world of "victimhood," which they have come to identify with.

Prevention and Accountability: Trust Is Earned

How could this have been avoided? First, trust is earned, and should not be given until it is earned. A system of accountability is designed to enable a person to earn trust. Trust is not given away; only license is given away. Trust is always earned incrementally: day after day, commitment fulfilled after commitment fulfilled, vow upheld after vow upheld.

Those who operate in the sphere of victimhood and blame are ready to protest any accountability with the statement "Don't you trust me?" Or the more manipulative version goes "You don't trust me!"—placing the one helping them on the defensive.

"Of course I trust you," they will respond. *Really? Why do you trust them?*

"Well, people need someone to trust them." Actually, they need supervised, accountable occasions to build trust that offer greater potential likelihood of success, without the temptations to self-indulge, blame shift, and thereby break trusts that they are supposed to be building. So often, trust is given by those with helping gifts without the necessary supports of structure and accountability; those supports build character and protect this person from themselves until they have learned to navigate in a faithful course over time. Only after this is successfully achieved and maintained over time through the appropriate structures of accountability can trust be earned and circumstances adjusted accordingly.

Micro-Bus Plan

So, our micro-driver friend should have turned in the money from day one to Bako at a specified time and place. They should have reviewed how many miles were driven, how many trips, and the cost of fuel, etc. Were there any challenges that arrived over the course of the day? Can things be done better in the future?

Only after following this protocol, the driver could then be paid his wages for the day. This should be done for the first four or five days to determine if the driver can be trusted. If there are significant fluctuations in earnings, it may require spot checks to observe if the driver is actually driving or correctly reporting income and expenses. Failure to return the vehicle on time (and similar behavior) will terminate the arrangement.

Where Is the Grace?

Many ministry leaders will balk at this kind of scrutiny and accountability. "Where is the grace?" they will ask. Grace is for the forgiveness of sin; it comes from Jesus Christ and is attributed to those who receive faith in Jesus Christ. Accountability is the grace that we receive in social relationships. With such social kindness we receive what is beyond that which we have earned through prior demonstration, and it is beyond what is customary.

Without this accountability, grace in these situations turns into license to sin, which is dangerous to those starting a renewed path before they have matured and earned it. Grace is not giving a loaded gun to an angry child, or a sportscar to a teenager. It is not grace to give what may be an ordinary thing to a responsible person but what is a likely temptation to someone else that can harm them and others in the process.

Therefore, ministry leaders and pastors should not be running the day-to-day of any business enterprise, even those related to funding the ministry. This "double duty" presents a conflict of interest, pitting two different gift sets against each other and jeopardizing both in the process. The livelihood of the businesses will conflict with the ministries that are supported by the profits derived from the businesses.

These can be hard tasks for those with helping and encouraging gifts, so if it is not to your liking, delegate it to someone who can perform the task. But trust the leader to whom you are delegating to run the supporting business well and appropriately. They should be free from attempts to interfere and turn the business into a charity. Likewise avoid giving trust to someone who has not earned it and has the propensity to squander the assets of an organization, whether charitable or otherwise, in unfaithful service.

Caution

In this scenario the ministry leader is taking a huge risk to the organization and their own reputation. The aspiring servant who desires to earn trust needs not only a manager but a person who can be a point of appeal, if they have a complaint about a lack of trust being demonstrated to them, or accountability structures that are frustrating and seem unfair, and so on.

This is where the ministry leader can be a helpful point of appeal, giving understanding to our frustrated worker who is on a path of recovery and productivity. In this place they can support the business manager and comfort the frustrated worker: "I know this is hard for you and you want more trust, but that must be earned. Your supervisor cares about you and your success. These structures are here to help you. Follow them and you will succeed. I believe in you. You can do this." This is the proper role for ministry leaders.

Point of Appeal

When the ministry leader places themselves in the direct supervisory position, the aspiring servant has no point of appeal. The ministry leader becomes boss, judge, and jury. However, with a separate manager in the business, our employee can have an appeal to the ministry leader as a last resort, where they can be heard, comforted, and assured that this is necessary and all in keeping with helping them build trust. Without any layer of appeal, the aspiring servant feels trapped, with nowhere to go. This can be wildly frustrating for those navigating their way to an improved and healthier life.

THE PRINCIPLE

This is one of our principles in our organization: *Do not let the pastors run the business.* They tend to run the business like a charity as opposed to a profitable enterprise. One cannot give away profits from the business to the ministry that are never earned, and worse yet, one cannot give away profits when the assets used to earn those profits are squandered and devalued.

Giving a responsibility beyond a person's ability is not a kindness—it is a burden and a cruelty leading to failure and disappointment, and one under which they may well fail. Those who placed the responsibility with them bear responsibility and accountability for creating these kinds of failure scenarios. As leaders we stand convicted if the burden proves too heavy for them; it reflects on our judgement and perception, and no one else's.

Objections

Returning to the bus scenario, what if the driver says he cannot come with the day's receipts because he has other pressing matters? Kindly insist, and if that fails, then retrieve the vehicle and end the driver's position. Second, third, and fourth chances are not grace—they are a pattern of forgiving without repentance and fomenting abuse of the opportunity and resources that have been entrusted to them on a limited basis. We dare not bless this kind of behavior. It is misapplied compassion. "But they have been through so much," one may say. Yes, and we are slowly building their confidences and strengths through successive opportunities for success through accountability, building trust and confidence one level at a time.

Standards Explained

When operating charitable organizations and churches, we are not obliged to throw away reason, accountability, and pathways to success. When laying out the requirements to the new driver, again state when the vehicle and the earnings are to be brought in each day. The vehicle is to be parked at the business, not to be kept at their residence or another alternate location.

The protest: "But it is a long way to walk."

The belief: "My employer should provide me with personal transportation."

My reply: "Lots of people walk every day. Perhaps this is not a good opportunity for you."

Reasons: It is not the driver's vehicle, and letting him keep the vehicle sends the wrong message about the organization. Do we provide transportation to all our employees? If they receive free transportation, they will assume the following: "I guess they do not care that much about their vehicle, and all the other employees are suckers for not getting free rides. And the larger community? Why is the valuable asset sitting here near our homes? Do they not care about such an expensive asset?"

A question to consider: Does everyone in your ministry or its supporting businesses get a company vehicle to take home every night? Unlikely. But what if they live so far away? Jesus is their Messiah, not any of us. God has his ways of making connections for people to overcome difficulties. You and the bus are not his only option. Let Jesus do the saving—not you. Until then, walking will build character and give them time for reflection and prayer. It may inspire them to find another job that is closer or motivate them to start their own business.

Grounding Questions:

- *Question 1*: Do you provide rides to everyone who works for you?

- *Answer*: Well, no, but he is going through a hard time.

- *Takeaway*: Hard times teach us character. They build us up and show what we can handle as we go in a new direction.

- *Question 2*: Are you prepared to offer transportation to everyone you work with?

- *Answer*: Well, no, they have their own transportation.

- *Takeaway*: Good, that is what we want to teach this person as well, to earn their way.

20

The Types and Levels of Managers

MANAGERS AND LEADERS ARE not all created equal. They come in a variety of forms and abilities, and they grow over time with training and increased responsibility. Each of these different levels and categories relates to the organization, its leaders' growth, and their ability to expand and multiply in dynamic ways. It is vital to long-term growth, expansion, and capacity.

Without these key managers representing different abilities, organizations will stagnate in growth, and their full potential will be unrealized. Many creative leaders will try to get by without a manager, only to their detriment as they toil away at tasks outside of their giftedness, robbing the organization of their best and underutilizing potential resources that could move them dynamically forward. In this and following chapters, we will take a look at essential types and levels of managers.

ESSENTIAL MANAGER TYPES AND LEVELS

1. Managers of self.

2. Managers of the business and organization.

3. Managers of employees.

4. Managers of the leader and his/her time.

5. Managers of the vision.

6. Managers of a multisite/multilocation organization.

#1: MANAGERS OF SELF

"No one told me I had to do that. No one reminded me to take out the trash."

When my children were young and learning personal responsibility, they regularly made these statements and others like them, as most children do. The implication was *I will do what I am told to do, when told to do it.* This begs the question: Did they consider doing the chore and put it off so that it had to be accomplished by someone else? (In effect, I interpreted their behavior to mean, "If I feel like it at the time, I will do it. Otherwise I might delay and forget, but not intentionally. I just forgot.")

A family teaching resulted. *Part of the chore is the job without a reminder.* That is, remembering and being accountable for completion of the chore is part of the job.

"I just forgot. I was busy. I didn't mean to forget. I will do it later." If my kids responded in that way, I would suggest to them the option, "You can hire me to remind you."

"What?" they replied.

"Yes, for five dollars I will remind you of your chores, and each time I remind you, it will be five dollars."

"No way, I don't want you to remind me," they said.

"OK, I was just offering. . ."

The reality of life, I would tell them, is that those who can manage themselves are paid more, and those who require others to manage them will earn a lower wage. If a person cannot self-manage, someone must be hired to manage them, and part of their pay will need to be paid to the person required to manage them. If you cannot manage yourself, part of your check will always go to someone else. You will be paying other people to manage you. . . whether you realize it or not.

Hire Self-Managing Employees

Too many times in organizations we are extending precious resources to "manage" poorly performing employees into better behaviors. The cost for this is high, and it rarely, if ever, pays off. When hiring an employee, we want to look for those who can self-manage the work assigned to them efficiently and promptly. We create systems to make sure the workflow is as seamless as possible, so that tasks can be completed expeditiously and so employees are not without resource or waiting for things that they need to complete their jobs assignments. Many managers of employees make the employee's work more difficult unnecessarily, as they parcel out resources with excessive frugality, frustrating the worker by constantly asking for approvals and provision while reducing productivity.

Self-managers are a blessing to organizations. One can rely upon them, and when they are on the job, the owner, boss, suppliers, vendors, and customers are at peace. They may cost more to hire for their salary, but they are cheaper because they require little or no supervision.

A good business practice in ministry organizations, businesses, or other industries is to calculate the amount of management time that a given department and its employees respectively require. Determine the breakdown; sometimes very few people require a great deal of oversight or things will go awry.

Other times it will be discovered that an employee is over managed or micromanaged out of productivity by a destructive manager, who just likes assigning random tasks on a whim without any regard for the employee's productive workflow. In this case the manager needs to be retrained, reassigned, or removed, in that order. Many of these dysfunctional managers are difficult to maneuver around, as they are publicly winsome and agreeable but intractable and dysfunctional as a supervisor. They demonstrate little change over time, do not respond to corrective action, hide their behavior and struggles, fail to appropriately report progress, and are the cause of multiple resignations of those they manage. This can be harder in ministry situations or nonprofits, where they have garnered a supportive group who like them but are not burdened with the frustration of working for them.

Self-managers regularly work out their own conflicts and will require little assistance. However, they will require the leader's support in the cases of extremely under-functioning and dysfunctional employees, board members, people with anger management problems, or whatever the case may be. However, in these circumstances, they tend to work toward resolution and healing even if the circumstance requires humbling themselves and waiting for a more opportune time to dig deeper, bring healing, and seek reconciliation.

People who self-manage make your life and work good and pleasant; they are a blessing to themselves and others. In contrast, those who require constant supervision by a manager are excessively expensive when adding in the manager's time and attention on top of the wages paid to the employee. Many times, the investment does not make financial sense when examined objectively from this perspective.

#2: MANAGERS OF THE BUSINESS AND ORGANIZATION

All managers do not necessarily have employees, although they can. Managers of the business and organization take charge of the work. It might be a pig farm, where the manager appears as the employee, except they are purchasing the food, contacting the veterinarian, maintaining the fences and facilities, watching out for the piglets, and so forth. They are acting as the owner, in so far as they take the interest of maintaining and protecting the assets of the pig farm; it is as if the profit and capital were their own possession, and they would be personally harmed if there was a loss to the business.

This level of responsibility and integrity is not to be equated or confused with the fear of dismissal, although bad performance may result in the dismissal of one being unfaithful or neglectful in the task. Rather, this is a reflection of their character and ability to manage a business or department of an organization. This manager has the gifts, skills, and motivation to perform well, and they thrive in an environment where they manage and take responsibility for the entire operation.

This kind of manager has the capacity to move beyond simply performing tasks and following instructions, to executing activities sequentially and prioritizing tasks as needed that serve the larger picture of the pig farm. They anticipate what is coming next and what will be needed. They have extra boards for the fence waiting, and nails to attach them, should some come lose. They are not caught unawares but are prepared for almost any calamity, as well as maintaining the regular routines to bring the greatest success to the business. They keep the owner aware of upcoming needs so that the owner can plan in advance and seek the best deal for the required resources. Some purchases may be beyond the manager's control or expertise, but in time these can also be overseen by the manager of the organization. Such managers bring solutions to problems that the owner has not yet seen or anticipated. They are a blessing.

I am amazed how many people I have worked with who constantly bring problems to those they work for, without bringing solutions, as if no one else ever saw the problem before. That is why we hired them in the first place: to be a solution person, not just a problem reporter. Identifying, managing, and correcting problems is what a good employee does.

The corrective is to request that the employee come with a proposed solution along with any problem reported. To improve their problem-solving skill set, ask the employee what potential solutions they have and how they arrived at those solutions. Then discuss the ideas, and potentially enhance them with stages of approach depending on the nature of the problem. Give the employee the lead in this process as they learn to ask the right questions in order to find solutions that bring resolution.

#3: MANAGER OF EMPLOYEES

The next level takes the above skills of the manager and combines them with the utilization and deployment of human resources. This is a different skill level that not all leaders or managers can achieve. Many business managers have high standards and are frustrated with the inferior work of some employees who do not share their level of dedication and excellence. It takes time to acquire the skills necessary to do certain tasks with excellence and complete them in a reasonable time frame as well, and some managers, after learning a skill over time, are frustrated with the speed with which others are learning the task. They may be tempted to step in and show how quickly they as the manager can perform the task. This does not inspire anyone.

Managing employees means that the manager is responsible not only for the completion of tasks through others but the relational environment and culture those employees have with the following: (1) each other, (2) customers, (3) vendors, (4) donors, (5) the community at large, and (6) the manager themselves.

Building a Healthy Workplace Culture

This can be a tangled web of relationships. If something goes awry in any one of these relationships, it can bleed into the other relationships and interfere with the ability of the organization to complete its tasks and goals. This is especially true if the employees or supervisor are from the same family, church, community, or ethnic or tribal group.

The bad relationships or interactions will spread like a virus and become increasingly difficult to correct if unchecked. Timely correction should accompany a clearly stated and expected improvement course linked to a specific timeline, followed by reassignment or termination of employment, as part of the correction process. Failure to take these steps results in workplace dissatisfaction and high turnover.

However, there are also times when creative job reassignments can be enacted so that an employee who is not thriving can be assigned to better utilize his or her specific abilities and temperament. This can avoid major realignments and personnel changes. The right person in the right place will thrive and be a blessing. Retrain. Reassign. Replace.

Illustration: Look at the Files

In reviewing documents from a preschool, the nature of the employees quickly became clear. Some employees had thick, extensive files, filled with complaints, notes, letters of infractions, and corrections. Other employees had a few kind words after many years of service where the files were very thin. The employee with the massive file included a final letter of dismissal for an infraction against the school's gossiping policy.

Policies and procedures lay out expectations and allow them to be communicated effectively, efficiently, and consistently. They provide a backstop against employees saying they were not aware and a consistent, recognizable standard for all working together. Unfortunately, many organizations "assume" these values without codifying them in writing. Until they are written down, they do not exist.

EMPLOYMENT AS A MEANS OF MINISTRY

One of the dangers in running ministries and nonprofits is the temptation to allow employment and the ministry function to overlap. We hire people to perform tasks that are required, not as a means of therapy, rehabilitation, or some other form of improvement. A director came to me once with an application from a potential employee. The applicant had trouble with the law, their credentials were not in order, and they self-reported financial management issues and a host of other challenges.

The supervisor of the ministry said, "We really need to hire this person and help them out. They really need help."

I countered, "They are clearly in a rebuilding phase of their life, but employment here is not therapy."

"But we are a church," she implored.

"Yes, and people come here every week going through great difficulties. That is the nature of a church, but we do not offer them all jobs on our payroll so they can get better."

I complimented the supervisor's big heart and compassion. Thankfully, she fully understood and supported our purpose and our values in helping broken people reform their lives—they just needed to be applied off the payroll.

Ministry is ministry, and work is work. The same skills that make a person a supportive person in ministry, if misapplied, can make them a weak manager, whose practices will undermine the very ministry they are trying to build.

Managers of people have a critical role, and failure can be catastrophic. In a school it takes only a single person to sow doubt into the whole organization. Parents, teachers, and children all become enmeshed in the problem, affecting even those who are far removed from the conflict.

As told above, one employee record I read indicated that the employee had been terminated from the preschool for gossip, a hobby undertaken by many at their own pleasure and peril. The file indicated that the school had a zero-tolerance policy related to gossip, and this was noted in the dismissal letter and file notation.

People with helping gifts regularly overlook these violations in an effort to support, encourage, and grow people to new heights. Unfortunately, those they are trying to help simply view this as weakness or acquiescence to their behavior or overall talented performance, and it remains unchecked. Termination is often the blessing required for corrective behavior to begin its course.

CREATE HEALTHY CULTURE

Managers of employees create cultures. They are keepers of the culture, and critical in this role is strong character, ability, and humility. Even the best leader can be undermined by an unscrupulous or self-serving manager. Some with more narcissistic tendencies can appear cooperative and supportive when they are with you, but in private they are countermanding your instructions and undermining you while working people against each other. All the while they profess to be the only one who is protecting the other person and the organization. These people are manipulative and wreak havoc among relationships as they build an appetizing dessert spread—with lies on top of doubt, sprinkled with "confidentiality" as their cover—over a long period of time, if given the opportunity.

Many Faces, Same Story

Another preschool director of many years played a rather covert, narcissistic game of having a unique face for every group they encountered. They assiduously played each group against the other, maintaining themselves as the "holy one" protecting them from the "problematic other," whom everyone needed on their side in order to survive.

When speaking to the preschool board, they would assert that "they were holding things together" for the board, while recounting how difficult the pastor and the teachers were. When meeting with the pastor, this director would say, "You know, the preschool board only has these two women who have been there a long time and really provide no real support. And the teachers are always making trouble. But I am here for you."

Another time the director would be with the teachers and say, "The board lacks direction right now, and the pastor does not actively support the preschool. But I have been here a long time, and I will protect you. So don't talk to them—they are just looking for ways to get rid of you."

In each case the person or entity being spoken to was subtly embraced as a friend in jeopardy, the other parties were presented as dysfunctional and potentially malevolent, and the director was the savior. They, of course, did the same with the parents.

For years the director continued in the patterns of self-interest and playing people against each other as they pleased. The director was finally called to account in a meeting about a mutual program with the church, where she apologized for missing the other meetings due to "urgent, last-minute circumstances." The pastor was calm and said that the director needn't worry. The director seemed relieved, and the details of the event were reviewed.

Just before exiting, the director apologized again for being late, saying they were sorry to have missed the prior meetings. The pastor then uttered these words: "The meetings are not really important, neither was this one, whether you are late or on time or come at all. Because as in years past, you will proceed to make last-minute changes and do whatever you want because that is what you always do. It is clear to everyone, so go do what you do. It has already been anticipated."

The look of shock on the director face was palpable. It was as if the secret curtain had been torn. Mouth agape, the director stood there momentarily and tried to draw the supervisor back in with acquiescing charm, surprise, and even promises, but none were to be received. The director resigned within the next fourteen days, voluntarily. There were no other conversations between them or attempts at maneuvering and manipulating the board.

However, there was a concerted effort by the director to sabotage the lead pastor's reputation with the teachers. Six months after the departure—and a lot of relationship building between the teachers, the teaching pastor, and the board (uninhibited by the departed director)—there emerged a new unity even among staff who had been there many years.

"We were told you wanted to close down the preschool," one of the teachers said shyly. "We were advised that we should leave and find other jobs before we were all fired." Such is the legacy of these kinds of people in management positions who have narcissistic tendencies.

Two years later, parents from the preschool started attending the church after a new director began implementing a vision to reach the families for Jesus Christ through a strong, loving preschool program and a prayerful partnership with the church. Many came to faith in Jesus Christ because of this shift in leadership.

Sub-Note

How does this sort of thing occur? It has a lot to do with the organizational culture, staff, and management, as noted above. This organization went through twenty years of tumultuous times with a series of short-term leaders, before stable leadership came that brought about long-term change and reversed what had been a steady decline.

21

The Manager of Leaders

THE NEXT LEVEL OF managers are executive management people with particular gifts for managing high-capacity leaders through knowledgeable and predictive administrative support. They utilize organization structure and assignments that maximize each leader's potential and gifts while minimizing distractions, weaknesses, and deficits *through the alignment of assignment and gifts*. In this way the leaders' weaknesses do not become part of their primary area of operational focus. Rather the mutual gift pool becomes the assignable area of responsibility and task to maximize each leader's—and the organization's—potential and consequent output.

In addition to increasing the productivity of the leaders, a direct corollary of job satisfaction is achieved for all involved. The challenge is the leaders delegating the authority to perform this function. Many leaders are unable to benefit from this sort of opportunity because they are unable to give authority for scheduling and assignments to another person who is better equipped to handle it, thereby clearing their calendar of unnecessary work.

AUTONOMOUS, WANDERING LEADERS

Traveling with groups of high-capacity leaders from around the world on a regular basis, one will notice that they often wander off like sheep.

Accustomed to leading and being regularly followed on a regular basis in their arena of influence, they struggle to transitioning to following others.

Attending a conference, I pointed out a particular leader across a large auditorium who led a significant work in Africa. Most of those leaders were from Africa, so I said, "Let me introduce you all to him." They all agreed and said they just needed a minute and then would join. It took twenty-five minutes of grabbing bags, finishing conversations, consulting together, and so on before we moved. By the time we made it across the large hall, the introduction only included one of the leaders.

I could regale you with all of the intricacies of what each one found "important" to do in his own sight as a high-capacity leader, but suffice it to say that leaders make global decisions all the time and become so accustomed to that format that they miss out on other opportunities. They have the practice and discipline of following themselves and not being directed by others for maximum effectiveness.

If you want to lead well, you must follow well.

These talented leaders have their own agendas, work styles, and preferences; no two of them are alike. As they progress in leadership roles, they effectively surround themselves with other competent, gifted leaders who manage the things not in the leader's gifting as well as those that the leader can do but are of a lower priority for their role in the organization. Conversely, when a leader is personally involved in (instead of aware of) every aspect of the organization, their effectiveness begins to plummet, as the organization does not benefit from the leader focusing on the essentials that the organization requires in each season.

KEEP FOLLOWING THE PRIORITIES AS YOU LEAD

As a leader is effectively maximized around their gifts serving the organization, they continue to say yes to the future by clearly, kindly, and firmly declining the *good* in favor of the *godly*. I would commend a book called *The Tyranny of the Urgent* on this topic. So much can come our way that seems urgent that the important things are pushed out of the way, and our days are lost in a thousand busy details demanding our attention, pulling us away from the things that help our organizations grow. However, leaders who choose wisely are those following God, not the whims or fads or pressures to please other people.

The managers of leaders know the priorities of the leader (because the leader has expressed them), their place on the calendar, and their personal capacity. They know when the leader needs a break from certain things so that they can refocus and be replenished for what is ahead. Like tending a precious resource, the manager of leaders tends to the flock of leaders, cherishes their value, and protects them from harming themselves as well as from outside attacks. The manager of leaders is a precious asset, a voice to wisely heed, or else their gifts will go to waste—to the peril of the leader.

Caution #1:

There are certain leaders in organizations who are unaccustomed to or unwilling to benefit from a *manager of leaders*. Often driven by obsession over particular gifts they possess, they mistakenly believe they are the only ones who can perform these tasks. Making things less clear is that people within the organization often prefer the attention, contact, and importance of the leader doing these tasks on their behalf, thereby exacerbating and further depleting the "superhero leader's" ability to cope with the stresses of daily life. This ultimately contributes to a likely failure in a crisis because they have run their personal resources so low. We will explore this more in the next chapter.

Caution #2

If the manager of leaders becomes more interested in their own power than in the interests of the leaders that they manage, the entire system falls apart. This must be addressed swiftly. Terminate employment without delay.

22

Unhealthy Personal Management
(The Superhero)

I AM HERE FOR YOU

A YOUTH DIRECTOR ONCE gave every youth group member and fellow leader their personal home phone and cell phone numbers, encouraging them to call or text at any time—day or night—if they had a need. As the youth group grew, these nocturnal youth beings took them up on the offer, to the great cost of the couple leading the youth group. Every text and phone call was answered, at any hour. In time they also expected the volunteer leaders serving under them to follow their example of 24/7 availability as sacrificial servants.

As the load became too heavy for this couple, they celebrated the sacrifice but ignored feeding the needs of those serving under them to sustain them. They neglected even their basic need for time and presence with the youth leader to answer simple questions, in favor of being the 24/7 crutch for every youth in the ministry. One by one, the leaders dropped away.

Five different senior leaders in the church were assigned to supervise this youth director, and one after another arrived at my office saying, "Can I talk to you about something?" Each explained, "The youth director is unwilling to listen to anything I say and ignores any suggestion or instruction I give. I simply cannot supervise him."

Managers of leaders can have many titles, and they are a valuable and essential resource to guard against excesses and inadequacies that can adversely affect individuals and organizations.

After the youth director's departure, we came to know that when the couple were "burnt out," they simply switched off their phones for days or weeks at a time until they were "personally replenished." Then they would reactivate the same relational dependence cycle on themselves from the group, followed by burnout, then once again repeat the cycle of retreat and ghosting when overwhelmed. This was destructive to the youth in the group and stunted their personal growth and maturity to a very low level.

This youth director was a charismatic speaker and led many troubled teenagers to Christ. Every highly talented person has at least one significant weakness—pride, of course, being the most prevalent and treacherous.

When the youth director couple rotated back to my care, I sought to figure out who his trusted sources of authority were that he was willing to follow. Eventually it became clear that a particular professor at the seminary where he was studying was the authority figure whom he responded to. When there was any area of growth required to enhance the ministry work, it made sense to ask the youth director what this professor would advise. Since this professor's advice matched that of our leadership team, this became our path of influence while he served during his seminary years.

Humorously, the youth director reported back the great and deep wisdom of this professor, who instructed the youth director in the same ways that we all had, but now these ideas were new and radical paradigm shifts by an authority whom he respected. I congratulated the youth director on the many insightful plans and encouraged regularly reports of the inevitable progress on the strategic changes to be implemented.

What would you or your organization have done in this situation? Clearly, we could have done better and likely should have intervened sooner.

UNLIMITED HELP BY LIMITED PEOPLE

Another leader on one of my teams was obsessed with using the gift of "helps." This was regularly practiced by bringing particularly troubled students from a seminary to live in their home for long periods of time. This became nearly a full-time occupation, and the time and energy expended consumed their home life, which should have been a place of replenishment but was a place of continued interruption and service. This drain on their energy was significant and showed in their work. They could not submit to leadership in this area and claimed it to be "personal ministry" on their own time. The problem was that it was a major depletion and eventually took a tremendous toll on energy, causing great distraction as the troubled young people faced mental illness challenges, near homelessness, and a variety of other significantly emotionally draining issues.

Ironically, when these depletions occurred, they would come and seek counsel for solutions for their wayward housemates, hoping to find a way to keep the problem resident in their home while finding alternate means to address the problems these people had. This was wholly unrealistic. Eventually, we agreed that this couple would identify a mentor couple from whom they would seek counsel before inviting anyone to stay in their home. Although rocky at first, this system served them and the church well for several years.

Although we may be operating within our gifts, we are all limited in our capacity to perform on a constant basis, and all of us require opportunities to rest, recuperate, and reflect. Carpenters put down their hammers, bus drivers hang up the keys, but many pastors run on empty tanks, relishing each opportunity and the blessings of using the gifts God has given them—with abandon.

23

The Manger of the Senior Leader

NEXT IN LINE IS the manager who joins the team because they believe in the senior leader or their mission. There two types of *managers to the senior leader*. One is primarily there to support the mission, while the other is primarily there to serve the leader. They are largely indistinguishable from each other. They both want to see the leader achieve what they want to achieve and will be loyal to them in whatever agenda or mission they pursue. However, when the senior leader moves on, the one who prioritized the mission will stay with the mission, and the other will follow the leader to their next assignment.

These types of managers are truly a gift, and they seek your best at all costs. They defend you against negative speech and limit problems from unnecessarily arriving on the senior leader's desk as much as possible to serve them well. Some of the managers of the senior leader have their primary loyalty to *the organization and the cause* and not the senior leader of the organization. They are not good or bad; they are just having different primary alignments or allegiances, either to the leader or the organization.

MODERN-DAY ELISHAS

I have had one or two of these people in my life and truthfully could not identify which one was their primary allegiance at the time. One of the clear signs I observe in managers of the leader is they have little interest in supervising others; they see giving their emotional energy to managing others in the organization, apart from regular friendships that nourish them, as a depletion and distraction form serving the leader and mission they are devoted to.

This is not hero or idol worship. This is a person like Elisha to Elijah. They want a portion of your blessing. They are knowledgeable, and most of all teachable, and they want to be with you in what you do.

They will quiet those who disagree but have little interest in politics and office staffing, other than to protect the leader from it as much as possible—but not through a supervisorial role. They have a hard time relating to those who are not faithful to the leader and will imply how they wish that detractors and unsatisfied persons would move on and make everyone else happy. They value devotion and commitment and want to see it in others, and when they do not, they hope that these individuals could find a person or cause that they could be devoted to in order to have the kind of satisfaction they enjoy. In their deepest place, they quietly resent those who do not work to support the leader and simply wish and pray they will be silent or leave (preferably the latter).

NOT ALWAYS TRUSTED

Some boards, as they encounter this type of *top leader manager*, are suspicious of them because of the ties with the leader and their potential influence; therefore, they fear that this manager of the leader may not necessarily have the interests of the organization as primary. They are sometimes correct in their assessment, as this person will willingly and quickly leave to support the leader in their next place. However, their support for the leader should not be understood as not supporting the organization. In fact, the work they do for the leader helps build the organization through the leader's improved effectiveness. One is not the opposite of the other; they just have different emphases that ultimately benefit both the leader and the organization.

On a personal note, many of these managers of leaders have difficult home lives. One pastor who proceeded me had an assistant who performed this function for the leader to great and legendary effect. Her own husband was an alcoholic, struggled to keep a job, and brought an ongoing level of confusion into her domestic life, which she counteracted through the order she brought for the leader—that her husband could not receive. She was trusted by all the leadership and knew how to make the right calls to get things done on behalf of the leader without his personal involvement. Interestingly, the church sought to maintain the position over time but did not want someone with those talents or abilities in the position.

MANAGER OF THE LEADER: VISION-FOCUSED

This type of manger believes in the cause or mission being pursued. They can appear to be like the manager of the leader, performing different tasks on their behalf, but in the end, they primarily serve the vision of the organization in their heart. If the head leader departs, they will stay with the vision of the organization.

To the leader, they appear as a friend and may serve as a confidant, but the loyalty is to the organization and its vision. They defend the vision at all costs and at times may even seem insubordinate to the leadership because of this devotion. In the developing world, the respect given to leaders is much higher than in the West. Likewise the vision is held in high regard and protected. This is much less so in the West where self-advancement and individual opinion reign supreme. In the majority world, this is viewed as disrespectful—because it is.

Express and Articulate

It is key for these types of managers to clearly express the vision. Many are promoting a vision that they assume is shared by the community at large, but this should be regularly repeated and clarified. In many cases the "vision" is clouded and conflated with the past programs and practices of the organization, which may or may not be specifically related to the execution of the central vision today. Or it is also possible that the central vision may need to be revised, updated, and readopted by all.

We will explore adapting vision to a changing environment in the next chapter.

Essential Element V

Adopting New Models for Missions

Bless the Old, Pursue the New

24

Adapting the Vision in Changing Times

VISION FROM THE PAST

THE VISION LAID OUT before us was "to build a great church to serve the city." The vision goes back 100 years, and yet the city and its profile have changed demographically over those years many times. At one time, 10 percent of the city attended the church—3,000 of the 30,000 residents. They were homogeneously white, upper-middle class to upper class. In the early years, the community had been a place of horse racing and gambling houses. As more established families moved to the community to build large homes on sizable pieces of land, the gambling and prostitution were replaced by a women's club and a church—the only church in the town for over twenty years.

In the next phase, orchards and chicken farms were eventually replaced by housing tracts in the 1940s and 1950s. By the sixties, the premier school district and new, affordable housing were drawing many young families. By the eighties, people from Hong Kong (1985–1998) were attracted to the community, followed by an influx from Taiwan (1995–2010) and mainland China (2010–present).

During my time at this church, there had been a massive migration of Taiwanese into the city, and they were then replaced by mainland

Chinese. The overall Asian population exceeded 80 percent in the schools, yet the church of 100 years had only a single Asian family. The church wanted to maintain its status as the premier Evangelical church in the community, even while other churches were closing due to their long-time monoethnic nature, as they aged out and were being replaced by new churches formed to serve the emerging people groups.

The mainland Chinese came with a communist background and were suspicious of Christians and churches, as they were taught that the Christians kept guns in the basements of churches ready to attack the People's Republic government at any time. The pastor of the mainland Chinese church that we helped birth asked me to see the basement room just to prove to himself that there were no guns, and he later told me about the propaganda films he had seen.

VISION NOW

The work of this local church in this era changed and required a fresh look at everything—from architecture to programming and ministry emphasis. Being the "best" church meant little to those with no background in Christianity. They were not looking for the right church or the most orthodox church—they were not looking for a church at all. They were, however, looking for co-belligerents who had at their heart values of family, respect for elders, and pursuing an opportunity for good education for their children.

When we engaged these families as whole units instead of breaking them down by age group, and engaged in promoting our shared values like "honor your father and mother," we finally struck a chord, and the Holy Spirit started working as relationships were built around family, community, food, and raising young children to thrive.

VISION PAST AND PRESENT COLLIDE

For some who had been in the congregation for many years, seeking out educational resources for adult education meant finding the most educated scholars in the nearby seminaries for hermeneutical questions. This was the value they wanted to continue to grow, emphasize, and provide for the community. However, those new to the community did not know what a seminary was. Although they valued education for their children, they did not have a desire for a specific high-caliber, intellectually focused engagement with Christian scholars, nor were they looking for that kind of education for adults in a church, as they had never been to a church. This created a disconnection between what the church promoted as part of the church's self-identity and the needs of the community.

Ironically, the emphasis of PhDs bringing intellectual biblical education in this congregation only arose in the 1970s and early 1980s, but that was the church's heyday, and it stuck.

Colliding Visions: Past/Present

Keepers of a vision from the past, although very valuable, will regularly wrap and conflate the values of the past almost exclusively inside the practices, programs, and procedures of the past. Those things that walked hand in hand with the mission, vision, and values in a prior era become sacrosanct practices and the desired personalities and staff to reacquire for the present and future. In that era, they became the best at what they did, but over time they forget the true purpose of the vision and values that undergirded the then-useful practices. Over time, when the vision's values are forgotten and the organization goes into decline, it struggles to keep the outdated practices and programs alive and stops adapting and innovating new programs. These old programs then supplant the vision and become sacrosanct.

New Circumstances

Those coming from mainland China in the third wave of immigration to this community were not people of faith; although the church in China has grown rapidly, these were not the people coming to the community. They were largely ignorant of the church, including the most basic teachings or stories from the Bible and how they migrated into the culture and literature of the United States. For starters, they did not know who David and Goliath were, and the majority believed that Jesus and Santa Claus were both "made up" characters of the Christmas season. The community no longer sought or demanded seminary-level education in Christianity. They required bridge building, relationships, English lessons, and basic education as to anything Christian.

Note: Do Not Seek to Replace the Old Vision

It is not possible to replace the vision of a long-standing organization with a completely different vision. To do so is foolhardy, time wasting, and will cause harm to all. If the leaders' vision is completely different from the past, they should start a new organization. Let the dead bury the dead; their perceived assets are not worth the trouble.

In every project we participate in—whether in our local community through changing demographics and people groups, or partnering with an international student to help realize change in a community far away—we are encountering a need to access the vision and values of the group or community that we serve, and to build on those core shared values. We will explore this process in the next chapter.

25

The Old Vision and the New Thing

"See, I am doing a new thing! Now it springs up; do you not perceive it?
I am making a way in the wilderness and streams in the wasteland."

—ISAIAH 43:19 (NIV)

REBUILDING THE OLD VISION VS.
STARTING A NEW THING

MANY READING THIS BOOK have a vision to establish new ministry structures in the existing organizations where they serve to address long-standing problems that have appeared to be intractable. A caution in working to transition existing organizations is twofold.

First, it is important not to give in to the temptation of a *savior mentality* and be judgmental of the organization's past failures or inability to adapt and make change in response to the new and changing realities. Respect their past efforts and learn from the values that drove those successes and what they did, both the things that worked and those that did not work (so as not to repeat the failures).

Being seduced into trumpeting the failures of others as a means of enticing them to follow the "new way" you are called to lead is also a common error and will become a self-inflicted wound. Be humble and discreet while remaining mission focused. The assets they have and the gifts they have received over time are a blessing but are often so bound up in past practices that they are not an available resource for future plans. Also do not pejoratively assume that these resources will be coming from what would or could have gone to your new organization or initiative. God will provide in time what is needed. God regularly creates out of nothing (see the universe) so that God will receive the glory—not the creative reshuffling of existing assets from other organizations whose funds and resources you might be secretly envying.

Second, do not be seduced into joining these existing structures and thereby hoping to change them from within, and then secondarily the larger community, through new initiatives and plans. This is not a strategy that will speed progress along. Quite the opposite, it will slow things down immensely as these structures move very slowly to change. Changing an existing structure in order to create a new thing is what Jesus spoke about when he said that *you cannot put new wine in old wineskins* (see Luke 5:37–39). They simply burst because they have aged to a structured and more rigid form over time that will only change once it has broken apart and must start over.

RESOURCE TEMPTATION

The temptation for using an organization's existing budget as part of a "vision-funding strategy" usually exists because there appears to be an existing asset base that can be better used for your new initiative. Likewise, seeking to identify resources that we can readily access from these existing sources for our own agenda, instead of trusting God to resource what he has ordered, will only create strife with the existing stakeholders.

These existing organizations and denominations are built to do what they do, everywhere in the world, even if those functions are largely obsolete or ineffective. Changing their entire structures to refocus resources on new projects will be a battle that will occupy all your time in the hope of getting some small part of the resources that they have already committed elsewhere long term. God has more than enough—he can provide for the new thing just as the old thing was provided for in the past.

OBSERVER STATUS

If someone wants to join in a project as an observer, funder, or provide a specific service to the project, welcome that but do not allow their culture to overwhelm or suppress the new thing. *It does not work.* In this "new wine being placed in old wineskins" scenario, both entities will be harmed, if not destroyed. It is easy to observe an existing organization, business, or political organization and trust in its assets and influence. It takes far more time than imagined, yields far smaller resources than hoped for, and will require the new vision to be modified to fit the parameters of what they traditionally funded. Likewise, as this self-identified funding path is pursued, the organization's funding models and amounts will be imposed on the vision and thereby limit it by default, or by the slow encroachment of the organization's assumptions and standards onto what God has called you to.

God funds what he orders. Trusting in this and cultivating new opportunities and new donors is where living, dynamic faith comes into play.

Question: Do existing organizations ever change? The answer is yes. It could result from new, charismatic, energetic leadership and vision, which have the tenacity to stay and work through the long-term challenges of painful, slogging, systemic change. Yet, more often change comes as result of observing innovators achieving success, which the existing organization may then seek to emulate as their funders' and supporters' interests move to the new thing that God is doing. However, it is just as likely that the organizational insiders will oppose the new innovations as those of outsiders who do not understand their ways.

Most large organizations, corporations, and the like are not structured to innovate. They are built to refine and hone what they already do. If innovation is necessary, it will be hired from outside, or they will buy up the work of innovators. It is challenging to start new things, and it takes significant sacrifice; however, that is how they grow and flourish. Older, established churches and mission boards change very slowly—if at all. New organizations start slowly and offer little to no compensation or salary, but over time they will outgrow and outstrip the established groups.

Essential Element VI

Global Exposure for New International Leaders

*New Vision Exposure and Practices
for Western Partners*

26

New Thing, New Seed, New Soil, New Team

BURIED ALIVE

WHEN GOD CALLS A leader to a new thing, God builds a new team, with a new vision and new funding. Being planted as a lonely seed can feel like being buried alive, as opposed to blossoming into starting something new. Just a short while ago, one of these seeds was part of that flowering tree and now is in a strange, dark place buried alone. Welcome to the new thing that God is birthing.

God does not cut a giant branch from a three-hundred-year-old oak tree to start a new forest. God plants a seed far from the parent and places it where it can be nurtured and germinate. When the time is right, the springtime of germination will dawn, so it flourishes in the light and has space to grow, not overshadowed by old trees from the past that block the light and stunt its growth.

This is a fragile place, and almost anything can seemingly destroy the new sapling tree as is sprouts up. Yet it is incredibly flexible in the storms that come, and it is not easily broken as it weathers the adversity of its first seasons. It slowly strengthens and builds roots before it races toward the sky for many new seasons, becoming more and more established and fruitful.

THE WAY IT WAS

In 1900, 9 million pounds of ice were harvested from lakes in the United States. This feat was performed primarily with saws, carts, and horses. That ice was then stored in insulated warehouses and locally delivered to "ice boxes" in peoples' homes by the "ice man." Later, around 1920, refrigeration allowed warehouses to make ice, and the ice man delivered it from his horse-drawn carriage. By the 1930s, refrigeration encountered the icebox, and the home refrigerator replaced the iceman and the warehousing of ice.

The ultimate mission was not ice harvesting but food preservation. Ice was the means to that end.

For churches and other organizations, they can confuse a type of musical style, education, outreach, or foreign mission program with the goal of worship, evangelism, disciple making, and so on. Likewise, a local village will tend to conflate existing communal agricultural practices with growing food, which can be done in a variety of ways beyond what is currently practiced.

MANAGERS OF THE VISION

The fifth level of managerial scope includes managers of the vision. If they can be helped to identify the essential values of education, mission, evangelism, or food production, they can be a valuable advocate for the vision in the present time and not just promulgators of past times and previous practices. In the rapidly changing world, it is difficult to stay up to date with all that change brings. Hunkering down to weather the storms of change until they pass is digging the grave of your organization so that it will no longer serve its purpose in the present and become a mummy or relic of a prior era.

Those tempted to hunker down and survive are quite often people of passion and dedication; they are indefatigable in persistence when others have lost hope and left for a more comfortable place. Yet these other stalwarts have stayed for various reasons, to carry the torch for the old vision into the future, or because this is the place where they became Christians, or the place where they buried their child, or other such significant milestones. They are managers and protectors of the vision.

CHANGING HOW WE APPROACH MISSION

The ways that churches, NGOs, or nonprofits do their work has not changed significantly in over seventy years. So, as we introduce the self-funding BAM, locally led mission initiatives (versus long-term, foreign-supported missionaries) many things are different and lay outside the path that churches and organizations have gone down for a long time. Resistance is natural. Some resistance comes in the form of ignorance, assuming that a new way or organization is just a different title but that things will still be done as in the past. "We have been through partnership changes before," they'll say, "and organizations we support have changed the names of what they do in the past."

Yet, self-funding, self-led, and self-governing were the values that modeled the Three-Self church in China and India. As we develop the utilization and empowerment of local, indigenous leaders blessed with a transformative, foreign educational experience who can bring trans-formational change in a community, there is also an accompanying, if incomplete, history of turning over local leadership of churches and in-stitutions to the local leaders.

Lesslie Newbigin describes that process from his time serving in India and how they adjusted pastoral training to be delivered in the community, instead of relocating the leader to a geographically remote seminary for three years. In an interview from the early 1990s, he states that Western churches in the seventies moved from sending missionar-ies to begin to pay the salaries of indigenous pastors and leaders, seeing their contributions as more fruitful and economical than Western mis-sionaries.[1] But this model also had its weaknesses as it still depended on Western funding and created local economic inequalities, jealousies, and was not locally sustainable.

EMERGING MODEL

The emerging model is not to pay local leaders from the resources of Western churches but from the ministries and business enterprises that are planted locally. The goal is to raise the overall economic and spiritual level of the community so that they can build their own churches and

---

1. Crouch, "Lesslie Newbigin," https://www.youtube.com/watch?v=b5BO4oCUYXs.

pay their own pastors and leaders and send their own mission workers to pioneer new fields.

Not Bi-Vocational

A seminary leader heard about our work and said he, too, thought that it was a good practice to have bi-vocational pastors as a necessary alternative where salaries are low. Ironically, that is not what our model advocates. We are expanding mission and economic activities through business opportunities, *not* giving the pastor a part-time second job. We can explore salary structures later, but the seminary leader was again taking something that he already knew about (as in Paul being a tentmaker) and imposing it on this emerging model of community development and expansion, which depends upon indigenous business expansion and the other services that a community needs to thrive.

The goal here is not to find a second job for an already overworked pastor but to invest strategically in a local community through the creation of medium-size businesses and ministries, and the jobs that go with them, to thereby foment economic diversification and expansion. By doing this, those who are part of the local churches will be able to pay the pastor appropriately as they are employed and earning more.

LEARNING FROM THE PRACTITIONERS

Over the past fourteen years, we have observed what works and does not work to grow a community in a sustainable way. We have analyzed for the causal factors that inhibited or delayed the desired growth—not only those that needed to be deleted but also those that needed to be added. In most cases, the things that needed to be deleted were there to cover over the problem of a missing element whose source and solution could not be easily identified at first, or the cultivation thereof was too slow for the rapid pace demanded by Western thinking.

Often, it is the missing pieces that are the essential component in the equation, such as local, visionary, entrepreneurial leadership empowered with education in the West and the infusion of capital assets to achieve a locally funded, expanding, and fruitful vision.

Either deleting or modifying alone those areas that already exist will not make up for the needed addition of *supplying all the missing pieces.*

Likewise, as we have observed the need to identify missing pieces and have added them, we have seen the flourishing of projects to be locally successful in building a robust, adaptable model that works sustainably.

These "missing elements" that we have identified require a longer lead time to establish, as they require longer time-frame inputs for education and travel for the local leader, time to build a business model, and time to test it with a "proof of concept" project on a smaller scale. Additionally, we have discovered the need to be open to adding new initiatives along the way as things grow. These added initiatives are not completely separate from the initial project, but rather they build on the strengths of the original. Continuing to refine the vision through these strategic additions prevents us from ignoring the unfolding future and allows us to continue to capture the needs of today and tomorrow. In this ever-changing global landscape, we can create lithe, adaptable structures and organizations that are led on the ground locally in communities where they can respond to emerging trends quickly.

There is a system of ongoing learning and sharing of insights to this model. It is not just a conglomeration of old and new but a strategic empowerment of the best of both, under the leadership of those who serve their local communities.

27

Education of Local Leaders Through Global Exposure

"See, I am doing a new thing! Now it springs up; do you not perceive it? . . ."

—ISAIAH 43:19 (NIV)

NEW THINGS REQUIRE EDUCATION, exposure, exploration, emersion, and explanation that lead to transformation. Especially since there are so many old and new structures built into the interactions of this model, it is easy for someone to grab or delete a piece of it based on prior experience and assumptions. When something looks or sounds like something we are familiar with, there tends to be a stoppage in critical thought assessment and critical incorporations, as the new information is placed within one of the old known categories with its concomitant prejudices and assumptions.

Like the story of the blind men touching different parts of an elephant and describing what the animal is, we easily make extrapolations based on limited experience or known models. Hence, reeducation can be more laborious than educating an untainted mind. Abandoning prejudices and creating room for new categories and paradigms of engagement is part of this process, for local leaders as well as their partners in the West.

THE NEED FOR CHANGE: "SOMEONE SHOULD DO SOMETHING"

Government, the Easy Go-To

One of the most common refrains when people want and desire change, including in the developing world, is "The government should do something. . ." This small phrase begins (and too often, ends) almost all discussions about jobs, industries, roads, housing, electricity, water, hotels, and so on. This paternalistic worldview is then paired with the hopeless experience that people have with corrupt, socialistic forms of government, which impose themselves in every sphere with incompetence, corruption, and greed. Once the conflation of government as the solution is complete, all hope is lost, and a commiserating of the past failures and corruptions becomes the topic of discussion.

The strengths of governments are also their weaknesses. Governments by nature manage, but they do not create or innovate. A government can commission a tower and then hire a great architect and builder to create the Eiffel Tower in Paris. Commissioning is not creating. There is an unfortunate correlation between big problems, which are large and widespread in scale, and the assumption that a government should then be responsible to create the solutions and outcomes to make creative solutions happen. Unfortunately, the government is not creative; it is administrative.

THE HISTORY OF THE CHURCH CREATING AND PIONEERING INSTITUTIONS

Universities

In the United States, when there was a need for universities, Christian groups built schools—from Princeton University to the University of California, Berkeley. These were Christian enterprises in their founding.

Likewise, the Christians in the U.S. built innumerable hospitals long before the government entered the medical-funding arena because the church saw the need for these hospitals and caring for the health of the poor. Local leaders innovated, raised funds, purchased plots of land, and built the first of many phases of these great hospitals. They were then run by local boards, and only later did politicians see an opportunity in which they could join in to infuse cash and take credit, garnering support for their political careers by bringing money to these operations.

Governments tend to follow trends and then codify them whilst the politicians take credit for innovating what someone else accomplished. Once the government intervenes, little local control or innovation remains, and the price structure of an activity is no longer related to market demand. This happens in every country and industry, and it gives governments excessive control over the society, thus eroding the freedom of individuals lives. The power of the electorate then is the only potential factor that can bring balance in this equation long term. The only other option is raising up strong, ethical leaders within the church community to serve sacrificially in government office, dedicated to bringing about internal change and not use the office as their fiefdom of personal and tribal power. The temptation is always unto personal expansion and individual wealth building through corruption, which is an inherent danger when power, influence, and large sums of money fall into people's hands who are not steeled in virtue character, and accountability. Even these fail without accountability.

FRUSTRATION'S TIES TO GOVERNMENT

Frustration is directly related to the power, size, and corruption of government. That statement becomes all the truer however long people live under systems of expansive and invasive government control and corruption, commonly marked by low outputs and accountability. As the areas of creative influence in society are systemically stifled making people the hopeless and hapless victims of the state—resting all future hope in an invasive government structure upon which they must rely to act on their behalf—they become more and more subservient and helpless, pressing their hopes into future leaders.

Fears

Even where the projects are not to be interfered with by government or other outside forces, there will still be fears by local leaders that they will be extorted if the success of what they are doing is noticed. Likewise, Westerners will worry about accountability and about resources potentially being squandered, or lack of proper controls related to resources, income, and leadership. (Then ensues the paternalistic, stifling patterns of Western oversight and control.) Locals will fear the unknown, as many promises are made and not fulfilled; or when fulfilled, none of the promised good outcomes materialize in the manner anticipated, but instead unforeseen problems arise, which they must carry on by themselves lest they be accused of incompetence or corruption. Local leaders with experience know these pitfalls, and they want to be sure an innovation is not ignoring or sugar-coating the new difficulties that can come up, as well as what has gone wrong in the past.

Secondary Government Role

So, the role of government in innovation is a secondary role in the process of development and should not be made primary, nor necessary, if the project is to go forward. In a project in Nigeria, I was invited to make a brief address at the inauguration of the Door of Hope International, in Miango Village near Jos, that provided housing and employment for widows so they and their orphaned children could live together and afford school fees. During the festivities, several meetings took place, wherein the local paramount chief donated 50 hectares of land to the ministry, and the area government liaison promised $3,500 to the project.

None of these funds or donations were in the original plan, but they gave it a significant boost. The land donation happened more quickly than the other money promised by the government representative, which took more than a year and a half to arrive. The principle here is to say "thank you" for all pledges and commitments from whatever source, but only count on what has been received for immediate decisions. We get into trouble when we start counting resources not yet in hand and modifying our present plans as if they were. These funds are "anticipated" and show support for what God is doing, but they must not be relied upon in advance of actual receipt. Promises and conditions change, and we do well to adapt to the new realities that emerge along the way, as they teach us faith in what is to come and faithfulness in what we have received.

SADDLEBACK CHURCH AND GOVERNMENT

"The PEACE Plan" is Saddleback Church's model for partnering in a country with multiple churches under the leadership of a main church to lead change in that country.[1] The relationship with the local government is often by the government's invitation, and many presidents of nations around the globe have visited Rick Warren and his PEACE Plan team in Southern California.

They use a three-legged-stool model for project success: the church, business, and government. Each is an essential leg of the stool, and the projects will not go forward without all parties participating in a healthy way. Governments must pledge that they will not extort or obstruct new projects as a precondition to participating; if they are unwilling, otherwise the PEACE Plan strategy does not go forward for that country.

One of our partners in Cameroon is the co-director for The PEACE Plan in Cameroon. The PEACE Plan begins with training for local churches in the "Purpose-Driven Church" paradigm, which emphasizes the five marks of the church. This ensures a common set of biblical values for the work of a local church, and that they are not dealing with cultish or personality-driven churches. It also weeds out those who are only looking for a means of getting resources without any sort of accountability or mutual relationship, as many will simply drop out in the first year when there is no money immediately coming.

The second phase is to implement The PEACE Plan by *planting* churches of reconciliation, *equipping* servant leaders, *assisting* the poor, *caring* for the sick, and *educating* the next generation.[2] The PEACE Plan offers many valuable resources online, including a training calendar, coaching programs, events, and other opportunities. I highly recommend The PEACE Plan content for local churches, as everything is clear, biblical, and user friendly, lending itself to an empowering paradigm—to see communities transformed and lives changed as they give their lives to Jesus Christ and develop their God-given gifts.

1. "PEACE Plan Model," paras. 1–2.
2. "PEACE Plan Model," para. 2.

It can be sound wisdom to contact the local government officials for a similar commitment to what is outlined above for projects that one partners in. The local conditions and relationships, religious contexts, and other matters will play a role in how and what that relationship with the government will be and how it could unfold. In majority-Muslim countries, governments do not generally participate in projects with Christian groups. That being said, there is no uniform model that works in every situation.

One partner in particular was approached by a government official in a Muslim country and asked if he intended any building projects for the church. When the pastor said he was considering it, the official insisted that he come to his office and file a permit immediately. "We will not be accused of preventing any church's works in this area," he stated loudly. And the permits were given in advance of any drawings or proposals.

Essential Element VII

Growing the Project Through Phases

28

Start the Project

NOW THAT THERE IS a transformed local leader and board in place—along with a vision and partner churches—do not wait for someone else to innovate and begin what God has placed on your heart. There is a reason that God placed it on *your* heart! Do not limit the future of your project to a specific key partnership with the government, an NGO, or some other large donor. Likewise, be ready for any healthy partnerships that will move the vision forward without diluting or redirecting the main vision.

Create healthy, self-sustaining, and self-propagating structures of leadership and multiplication that effectively utilize budgetary and financial controls and generate local income. The latter is accomplished by establishing businesses and providing resources for others to start businesses, which bolster sustainability so the community's vision will not fall prey to failure in the future due to a lack of outside funds.

Local investments of capital to produce business opportunities—which will provide funding income for the ministries, jobs from medium-size businesses, and seed money for small entrepreneurs—create the stimulus for economic diversification. Once that takes hold, people joyfully take charge of their own futures in fruitful ways, starting small businesses and hiring people to help them. During these times of transition and expansion, we want to bless, inspire, and encourage those around us to pursue great things and resource them for success, to no longer live in poverty, fear, and desperation.

The point of this model is to do the work in a way that will get results and maximize the greatest number of peoples' potential through creative opportunities. The focus is on using their gifts to create new businesses and provide autonomy for their own lives, blessing their families and communities to bring about the outcomes that they desire. Empowerment, not dependency, is the goal. Expanding opportunities through reinvesting in those who are most fruitful and increasing their responsibility will bring about the greatest change—not investing equal amounts for all, which will quickly dissipate resources without a positive return on the investment.

29

Cultivating Healthy Partnerships

UNIQUE, HOPEFUL, FLOURISHING PARTNERSHIPS

EACH LOCAL SITUATION HAS its own uniqueness, and it is impossible to predict every potential eventuality with certainty. Being open to "happy eventualities" and joyously adding healthy, unexpected new partnerships is important and a blessing. Since there are no perfect systems for modeling that or predicting the specific outcomes and needs that will arise from the strong foundations that this model produces, one cannot always foresee the future partnerships that will be necessary. This model—which intentionally emphasizes the fostering of unique, local, creative vision and dynamic flourishing—is constantly open to what God is doing *now* and *next*.

As partners emerge that may not even seem to fit the current unfolding of the vision, consider these early introductions to where God may be leading in the future, and begin to prayerfully seek the guidance of the Holy Spirit. God does not always reveal the totality of what we are called to do in a project or in our lives because of our limitations. When the time is right, these things will begin to unfold. Do not worry if the new potential partnership does not fit your existing model; this is a foundation that God will build upon, so make it strong.

CHANGING PARTNERS—EYES OPEN

Each community development project ultimately takes on a life of its own. There are no perfect circumstances, perfect outcomes, or perfect leaders for that matter. Likewise, when relationships change and one partner moves on, it is not the end of the world. It is a changing of seasons. Planters move on; be grateful for the seeding. Teachers come and fertilize, while evangelists come and harvest—each in their season. This is not a time to drop your head in doubt and despair. Instead it is an opportunity to keep your eyes open and alert for another open door, for something you might not have ever considered, or decided was not going to happen when it did not materialize early in the process. Keep your eyes open for the "new thing," especially when you are tempted to give up because of what may have been lost or ended in a particular season.

When God wants to bless something, he does it in unpredictable ways that clearly demonstrate his unique hand of blessing, as he weaves together things that we could not have imagined or created on our own. When our last potential blessing seems to have walked out and closed the door of opportunity, and we feel alone and desperate, suddenly there is a knock.

". . .As the Lord has assigned to each his task. I planted the seed, Apollos watered it, but God has been making it grow. So neither the one who plants nor the one who waters is anything, but only God, who makes things grow. The one who plants and the one who waters have one purpose, and they will each be rewarded according to their own labor. For we are co-workers in God's service; you are God's field, God's building" (1 Corinthians 3:5–9).

30

Doubt and Disagreement
The Companions of Effective Change

THE PROJECT HAS STARTED, and things are beginning to take shape as a new ministry is growing. The community is starting to be transformed. The more things change, grow, and improve, two phenomena will happen that are diametrically opposed. First, the leader, who is pouring body and soul into this fruitful project, will start to get tired, trying to keep it all going, and will hope for encouragement from those who are being blessed. Second, those who are being blessed will start to complain about how things are different, what has been moved, and what is no longer the same. They will sow *doubt* that leads to a crop of discouragement and matures into a harvest of *disagreement*.

HARNESSING DOUBT AND DISAGREEMENT

These two are natural responses to change, indicating that people have healthy minds and that they are alive, thinking, and engaged. It is good that people in the community are noticing the positive change! How we direct their questions and concerns towards the positive future we are working towards will affect the long-term success trajectory and outcomes of the change and transition that we are striving for. This will significantly be influenced by how we handle these two culprits that regularly emerge in the midst of making new things. Otherwise, if not handling them appropriately, we will usher in a season of disagreement and *dissension*, which will be toxic to the project and the people involved.

Doubt indicates that it is time for a refreshing and restating of the vision, as in Nehemiah, when the people forgot the purpose of building the wall of the city within four weeks of beginning the work. Disagreement, meanwhile, is to be harnessed to embrace the vision in refreshed and renewed ways. We do well to answer the frequently voiced questions, to display what we know while being open to the future. We will forge new roles and relationships as emerging leaders are identified by their commitment. Others will be assigned to lesser positions of influence over time as they max out their leadership capacity, demonstrating an unwillingness or inability to put doubt aside and strive positively into the next level where God is taking things.

There are some great people who help break ground and lead early on, and leaders will often envision them going all the way with them to the end. But some simply are not designed or equipped to lead in those later stages and will start to demonstrate that through their doubt. After careful observation, care, and revelation, we owe it to the vision to bring in those who have the capacity for what is next. Fruitlessly tying the vision's ultimate fulfillment to those who cannot make the advance to the next level is a disservice to them and to the vision. Some of these leaders are planters, and they will find the next vision to plant, playing a founding role as that new entity also gets off the ground in its first stages.

LEVELS OF DOUBT AND DISAGREEMENT

Beyond the confusion of preserving the past and fearing the future (i.e., doubt)—or highlighting a single struggling aspect of the new structure and process to say that the whole thing will not work (i.e., disagreement)—is a problem necessitating continued vision education. But there is also an opportunity for resolving confusion and misunderstandings through clarifications and concise, careful restatements of the vision as new circumstances and situations arise that demand them. And arise they will.

EARLY ADOPTERS

Early adopters will often take one of two paths. They will want to jump in and change everything right away or return to the early days of the vision and keep things at that place. It is important to understand the two dynamics and determine which is at play. Most doubt and disagreement are best treated as confusion and not as opposition (even though it feels like opposition). Becoming combative with doubt and disagreement only gives life to and reinforces the arguments being proffered by the "D&D" crowd, something we do not want to do. Anticipating the questions that people will have and including them in our presentations and materials goes a long way in diffusing confusion and the growth of unnecessary opposition. At the early stages of project planning, host a series of gatherings where questions can be asked openly. The frequently asked questions (FAQs) become the basis for honing future presentations and the communication of the vision itself.

Come up with a list of FAQs and provide answers to those questions. Make these available to everyone participating. Make sure the questions are presented in a reasonable, objective, and fair way, and then give clear and concise answers to address them directly. Ignore any personal invective or criticism; seek out the substance and answer that. Remember, people ask questions because they care. It is paramount that the leader does not take all questions as personal attacks on their leadership. Critiques of the leadership should be answered by others separate from the specific question that they were originally attached to. If someone is questioning the character of the key leader, handle it separately. For example, you could publicly state, "We want to thank Andrew Jr. again for coming and presenting this vision, which we all share. He has served our community for many years and planted the local church and school. He has shown his love for our community, and we are grateful to have him here tonight." Directly responding to character assassinations by mentioning them and responding only gives a second endorsing voice to foolishness. Allow foolishness to rest solely with fools.

IMPLEMENTATION

In this model of international community development through a local church partnering with established indigenous leaders who were studying for graduate degrees in the U.S., our student leaders were our ambassadors in both the local church and the partner church in their country. Their energy and enthusiasm naturally spread to people inside and outside the church, as they came into contact with high-capacity leaders from the larger community.

Spontaneous Support

People in the church were financially supporting the early phases of the project with resources to build the first two classrooms for a fledgling school, before the leadership of the church ever got involved.

Personal Confession:

As the senior pastor, I loved the students studying in the U.S. and invested in them personally as church planters and leaders, but I was skeptical about poverty programs and the potential outcomes of sending money to Africa and other poor regions only to see it disappear. I am a convert!

Note: The confidence of working with church planters was due to my prior and ongoing experience and success in working with international pastors locally in Southern California and in seminars, trainings, and coaching around the world. That experience also includes learning from and coaching pastors with church planting groups, coaching pastors globally from the Middle East, Africa, and Asia, as well as helping church planters from these regions start churches and multiply them in Los Angeles and around the world.

31

Adopting New Forms of Mission in an Established Church

POTENTIAL MISUNDERSTANDING— DOUBT AND DISAGREEMENT

Principle: Add Before You Delete

FROM A MISSION'S BUDGETARY program perspective, we did not do a wholesale partnership change. We merely added these projects as special projects that required raising special funds through campaigns separate from the budget. This was conducted along with what we were already doing, and support grew organically from the internal relationships with our leaders in training from abroad. Then we began to implement this strategy one community at a time in the developing world and watched what happened. We took careful notes and spoke openly about what was going on—frustrations, failures, miracles, and unanticipated blessings—all the while inviting prayer and learning from our challenges and mistakes. This kind of transparency was appreciated by everyone and made us all learners and students of the new thing that we were part of. In some years, our giving to missions doubled or more by the extra commitment gifts and reached 30 percent of our total offerings received.

This strategy was partly necessitated by the leadership of the mission committee being comprised of ten retired mission workers, who only supported giving to missionaries and existing mission organizations. They vociferously opposed any innovation or change in that policy. One of the challenges with separating too many projects from a general budget is that it teaches people to choose amongst the things that they are most passionate about, when the other underlying expenses to operate continue unabated.

So, what are the levels of *doubt and disagreement*? As stated above, some are confused, and some are picking at parts of the whole to prove that it will not work. Still others want to take a role of "positive" opposition to protect the ongoing mission work and what has been done in the past, in fear that the new will displace the old and cause harm.

But as we have seen, this is not a theoretical model. It is, in fact, a practiced model that is consistently bearing outsized fruit compared to our prior practices, and it will surely continue to evolve and bear fruit as time goes on. Again, some will disagree with this "new" approach because they fear it will jeopardize relationships with existing missionaries or organizations.

DIVINE COINCIDENCES

Interestingly there were a number of long-term mission couples who left the field and no longer needed our support as this initiative was gaining momentum and expanding. We did not highlight the transition other than to celebrate the faithful work of our mission partners over many years as they returned to the States. They came and thanked the church for years of consistent love and support, sharing their experience of service and what was next for them.

New Members Enthusiastically Embraced the New Model

Overall, our emerging partnership in community development/transformation was not viewed as pushing out the traditional partnerships, but there was a natural transition. For those new to the church, it was their most enthusiastic reason for joining, for it realized a passion they had for wholistically impacting a community for Jesus Christ through innovation and exploration—leading to lives being saved spiritually, physically, economically, and in every other way.

Added Value: Reach More Communities with the Same Resources

Over time the fruitfulness of this approach can influence how your church, ministry, or organization works with others. You will see how this work promotes natural independence through specific, targeted, strategic investment for growth and expansion with the outcome of multiplication and financial accountability. Since the funding duration is *limited,* this allows a church to impact many more communities in a positive, expansive, multiplying way than if they were providing monthly support on a dependency basis for years on end.

NOTE FOR YOUNG CHURCHES
WITHOUT A MISSION STRATEGY

Many young churches do not support international mission workers or mission work and are confused into focusing exclusively on local growth and evangelism. Here is an invitation to embrace the Matthew 28:18–19 call and strategy to simultaneously reach a local Jerusalem as well as a different culture nearby, and another still, far away. This is not sequential ordering; it is an all now and abiding instruction.

As God brings growth to this young church, people of passion will be raised up to impact the local community and the world. Failing to embrace what God is doing by supporting them will limit the growth and connections of young believers in the community. Encourage venues for gathering, and support those whom God raises up or brings in your door from abroad studying here—whether the funding is formal through budgets, or spontaneous through special offerings, or an annual "first-fruits offering." Embrace what God is doing however that may be done, and abandon the spirit of poverty and self-interest of a fledgling church "surviving" instead of thriving and living up to its fullest purpose as it serves God locally and globally.

For those implementing this community development strategy as communities transition, the same principle applies. There can be a fear of losing existing relationships and offending current partners, as well as doubt as to the efficacy of what is being proposed and enacted. Many of these initiatives and new practices will be initially embraced by some (early adopters), and others will take years to adopt and implement them and will join as they see the success and fruitfulness of others. This will allow them to begin to abandon the scarcity, poverty mentality and the security of doing small things with minimum risk and maximum fear—which drives the constant embrace of "doing things the way they have been done"—to finally beginning to overcome and replace this short-term, survival way of thinking, planning, and living.

WESTERN DISAGREEMENTS

There can also be larger disagreements where this becomes a turf war over who is in charge and what model is best to follow. Local leaders of a mission committee or social justice network may see a threat to their past practices or leadership, or the long-cultivated leadership of outstanding partnerships. Yet these do not produce the same kinds of fruit as empowering local leaders and peoples, which costs 90 percent less and yields greater fruit.

Village Leadership and Foreign Leader Interactions

The local stakeholder leaders of a village may also question whether they are being adequately respected and consulted, or if someone from outside is trying to pull the strings from afar and usurp their local leadership autonomy once again. In reality, because this model necessarily relies on empowering and resourcing local leaders, that problem is greatly diminished over a comparatively more standard Western model of foreign leaders entering a community, trying to quickly implement partial solutions to complex problems with little input from local leaders, and functioning as outsiders living in walled compounds far from the village. The flourish of narrowly focused and defined activity controlled from the outside happens relatively quickly, yet the foreign workers spend years trying to establish relationships of credibility while immediately implementing monthly resource-dependency solutions, bringing outside resources and little long-term change.

Again, when someone comes from the outside, many locals will think the suggestions being proposed are fine for where this person is from but will not work in their community. In general people want the benefits without the cost or pain of change; that is the human condition. It is all the more prevalent when so many from the West come and go and seem to leave things worse than when they arrived when all is said and done. They have no model for truly empowering local leadership, authority, and decision making, which will bring about locally sustainable employment and business opportunities.

WHO IS IN CHARGE?

God is the one in charge, but the Holy Spirit is regularly thwarted by those convinced of the efficacy and necessity of "their standard method" as opposed to the empowerment and insight that comes from mutually humbling ourselves to each other and God's authority, expressed through our following and leading in obedience and congruence with God's unique plans and purposes for each community. Therefore, encourage prayer and proceed perceptively, faithfully, and proactively. The greatest experts on a community are the ones who have lived there their whole lives. The greatest authority resides with the one who created and loves them and will never leave them. The rest are a distant third place.

MISSION COMMITTEE RESISTANCE

The local church's mission committee that reluctantly undertook experimenting with and implementing this new model was made up of 80 percent retired missionaries when we began this journey. Their exclusive and stated agenda was to use all funds to go to missionaries serving in the field. They discouraged short-term mission trips by our youth and others as "taking vital resources from full-time mission workers," making it clear they would not fund such endeavors in their budget. This opposition to mission trips remained true for them even if the youth and adults raised their own funds outside of the budget of the mission committee. This is not reported to disrespect the work that missionaries have done for decades around the world.

Stages

However, there are different stages to any mission endeavor. That includes the pioneering mission workers, who cut through jungles and crossed deserts to reach isolated people groups. Over time, a teaching and discipleship ministry becomes the dominant form, and then creating a self-sustaining local work that covers every stage of life, maturity, education, and its own mission work. Likewise, we build and mature local emerging generations in the contexts of passionate mission workers, supporters, and engagers.

Scarcity Mentality

The cup-half-empty mentality—which seeks to reserve all current and future resources for current activities without consideration for future recruitment, growth, and expansion—fails in the Western partnering countries, just as it does in developing countries around the globe. It is a scarcity mentality, which for many of these retired missionaries was born from their genuine experience of significant sacrifice while lacking access to the resources necessary to do what they believed that God had called them to do. Instead of seeking a bigger piece of an existing pie, we must grow the pie and bake more pies. This can only be done by creatively expanding the pathways for resources and engagement beyond the existing structures and pathways.

32

Working Yourself Out of a Job

PHASE 1

RUTH WILSON SERVED AS a missionary in Sudan for three decades, teaching young girls to read and write. These girls were excluded from attending school, and as Ruth went about from villages and cities, she brought a new realization as to the importance and efficacy of women's literacy. She served well into the 1970s, when her work ended as the government's policy changed, based on the fruit of her decades of work, and made education available and required for girls.

PHASE 2

Thus, her original mission was accomplished.

PHASE 3

Subsequently, Ruth went to the Evangelical Theological Seminary in Cairo and taught others how to bring literacy to children in other countries where that was not yet the case. This was how her mission work matured and progressed.

PHASE 4

The final phase of Ruth's work took place after her "retirement" and was to support new mission work and church plants for immigrants to the United States. One example was the Arabic Church of Temple City, California, including its television and online broadcasts of the gospel and publishing arm. Pastor Hisham Kamel told me once that Ruth was one of the faithful monthly supporters who gave out of her small retirement to see new things planted and thrive. This started in 1990 and ran through the 2000s as God gave Ruth many years well into her nineties. Pastor Hisham also informed us that Ruth had been one of his beloved professors when he was in seminary in Cairo in the 1980s. God is indeed good. We always do well to follow what God is doing in each phase as it grows and matures, instead of clinging to a fruitful season now past.

TAKEAWAY

Imagine the plans that God has and how the Holy Spirit is working them together to accomplish and achieve things that we cannot envision decades—or even a hundred years into the future—before those who will be leading and serving in them have even been born. As one prone to anxiety at unfulfilled plans, I find encouragement in this to see God at work in sovereignty and purpose, weaving together a tapestried future that covers more than my current struggles but the worries and woes of the world. Consider how has God blessed *you*. He has connected you to people and resources that you could not even think to dream or pray for, and yet they appeared just as they were planned, often arriving after a challenging, tumultuous change that seemed like the end. But it was not the end. It was just a period in time, a season and a small space before the next chapter of blessing and opportunity was to be written.

33

Obstacles

Structure, History, Future, Power, Familiarity

OBSTACLES WILL ALWAYS BE present in various areas and categories, including organizational structure and history, as well as notions concerning the future, power, and familiarity. These are just some of the things that will slow down the church, ministry, or organization implementing a model of local leadership and economic empowerment to those transforming communities globally. You will also encounter regular opposition, complaining, and lamenting about how things were in the past before all these changes happened. Welcome to working with people. This is a positive sign that people are feeling the change, things are shifting, and this is not how it used to be; otherwise you would hear how nothing is really changing and how people are frustrated at the slow rate of progress.

We hope for affirmations and direct encouragements from people as we lead them, but instead they give us signs and indications that tell us what they are perceiving. Thankfully, God accepts us where we are, but he never leaves us to stagnate in our own juices.

TYPES OF DISAGREEMENT

Local Knowledge

"We know what we are doing!" Scenario A: "We have been living here a long time. Do not try to change us if you do not know what you are doing." Scenario B: "We have been implementing this new change now for some time. We are learning and trying. Please do not treat us as novices anymore."

Perceived Competition

This is a my-program-versus-yours mentality. "We have learned over time, and we do not want to dislodge and lose what we have already learned. Perhaps we can add some of what you bring to test it."

Trust on Both Sides

Scenario A: "How do we know you will stay and not simply abandon us as others have in the past?" Scenario B: "How do we know these people will be faithful and accountable with these resources? What is our guarantee?"

Trusted History

Scenario A: "This relationship with mission organization 'X' has been operating for a long time. We have a good track record of support and understanding with this organization. We do not want to break ties." (We can say the same about the local empowerment model expressed here as well, but it may likely be a track record not yet shared by others who are new to this model.) Scenario B: "This is our cultural way of doing things. We are unsure of embracing new things that may cause us to lose our identity by being subjected to the ideas and ways of others."

Unequal Comparison

"Others who have tried this have failed." The implication is, "So will you. Why are you any different?" This is usually a misnomer, as someone or a group may have tried an aspect or certain parts of this model and yet lost the necessary local accountability and ownership, thereby missing out on the fruitful results derived from the full-length approach.

DEFINING QUESTIONS

The clarity of questions that we ask determines, in large part, the responses that we receive and the strategies, priorities, and partnerships to be pursued. It is generally not fruitful to ask, "Which groups should we cut off or terminate that are inefficient friends we are currently working with?" That tends to be a negative preemptive approach. If in time the continued work of empowering community-development projects bears fruit, then the model can be applied elsewhere in successive projects, or as necessary, shifts of resources over time will tend toward the areas of greatest fruitful return on investment. This is assuming there are not unnecessary political pressures at play in the culture, supported by noisy banner carriers. Nothing worthwhile is free from opposition; in fact, it is a proof that you are doing something worthy of notice.

Frame the Question

Question 1: Do we want to send $40 dollars a month to support a child for *fifteen* years, or do we want to transform a community in a few years by funding permanent, new business profit-supported educational spots for $40 a month for *one* year?

Question 2: Do we want to permanently impact a single child after fifteen years or sustainably transform an entire community after just five years in a fruitful, multiplying way?

Question 3: Do we want to send money year after year to feed a child and give them medical care, or do we want to equip their family to increase their income and pay for their food, medical care, and schooling themselves?

Questions Focused on Potential Outcomes

These are the real choices that we are making. We want people to be prayerfully informed to make astute decisions as stewards (investment managers) of God's gifts and resources, called to go into all the world and bring God's loving kingdom at every level to every person.

Our questions are focused on potential outcomes that impact the most lives, not a specific organization, history, or protocol. But yes, there is a protocol here as well, and one is wise to employ it, as this is not a model where parts can be added or subtracted without doing serious harm to the model and the ministries in the community, even if unintended.

PRACTICE THE MODEL TO FREE YOURSELF TOWARD SUCCESSFUL INNOVATION

When instructing apprentices in construction, we emphasize practicing each step of the process in the order and form instructed until proficiency is achieved. Only after that should one try innovating—after having mastered it as instructed. Most "untrained innovation" leads to unintended mistakes because the training and steps of the method are preventing the unintended errors that the apprentice has not yet considered that could be created by their premature innovation. Subsequent innovation after acquiring the proper skill set can be an improvement subsequently—but not before this acquisition of exercising the model.

Local Creativity

The model and practices described here cover essential elements for fostering local creativity, innovation, ownership, and success. Unlike starting a franchise of an existing system, these components foster a framework for adaptability to local realities in a healthy format that intentionally blesses essential creativity without stifling accountability for resource utilization and proportionate return on investment.

Utilizing these concepts and proof of concept projects—like building schools for girls or digging wells—are measurable, leveraged types of projects, based on return on investment and addressing specific challenges with anomalous consequences. They are part of a wholistic approach that is sensitive to and inclusive of these "crucial issues"; yet they are not exclusively limited to them as much as they are part of employing the undergirding principles, along with other efficacious project facets, to bring the highest results as well as participation and local ownership for project longevity.

The Western urge to get things done "as efficiently as possible" can then become a warrant for the temptation to skip the steps and principles that bring about these long-term sustainability results through local control and consequent flourishing of the community through this model. One does this to their own peril.

34

Deviating from the Model and Principles

MEXICO, MISSIONS, AND MONEY

ONE OF MY TEACHERS, Mike Kim, worked with me at a local church and began a mission work in Mexico. As it grew, it needed a building, and later an expansion and addition. For the first phase, Mike went down to oversee each stage of construction and paid for the completed work. Once the second phase commenced, having worked with the local contractor before, Mike decided to pay the contractor up front for all the work and did not visit the site regularly to see that the work was progressing according to plan. The contractor took the money, started to dig a small area for the foundation, and then had a series of delays with many excuses. In the end, the only things finished were the money, relationship, and trust. Future fundraising became almost impossible.

Principle: Only Release Funds for Completed Work

Mike phoned me later on—after I had advised him to stay with his prior practice of accountability, completion, and payment—trying to figure out how to get the project back on track and his money as well. I had little to offer, as the situation was already codified. Mike was deeply disappointed, hurt, and offended. He was considering completely closing down the project and mission work. He believed that the local people should have been more appreciative of his efforts and was stunned that people from the community would take advantage of his trust and good intentions in this way—by the robbery by the very ones who wanted to be helped and assisted in the community. No one in the community took Mike's side.

Although I advised Mike to remain faithful to the calling that God had for him and seek God's resolution for the project, he was unable to continue after this setback. Subsequently, Mike decided to abandon his participation in the mission project.

I was blessed to learn from Mike's struggle, and as a result, all our projects are led by an accountable leader from the community. Likewise, all work on construction or land acquisition is reimbursed after proof of completion is in hand and substantiated through receipts, invoices, photographs, independently verified deeds, as well as a local inspection.

Objections (and Answers)

"Well, it does not fit our current policy. We want to trust people." *Adjust your policy.*

"We are not sure it will work. How do we maintain control?" *You don't.* We give control away so people can flourish. This is coupled with a promise that they are responsible to make things work. No more money will come after the initial investment. There is no bailout fund. The business model must be followed and will determine success. We maintain accountability for capital investments and disbursements.

AUTHORITY, AUTONOMY, AND ACCOUNTABILITY

Future accountability is maintained because local failure to manage resources means the mission will end. No one is going to bail them out. They are adults and have primary accountability to manage what they have been blessed with. There is a business model, and it has set points for local income and distribution; if these are not being achieved, attention must be paid early on to make adjustments and get things back on track.

Responses

"We have never done it this way before." That is why it is called *new*.

"It will take too long to implement this model, to educate a local leader as a student and see them return home before we see any fruit." Yes, it will take more time up front, but during that time, you will get to know this person and build trust in the relationship. A fruit tree takes five years to be bear a good crop, but after that is grows exponentially.

"How can we limit the delay?" By doing things the same way and having less fruit.

ALTERNATE QUESTIONS: EXPAND THE VISION

Ask your partner thought-provoking questions like these: What are the initiatives we could consider that might improve our overall effectiveness in spreading the gospel and fighting poverty, to bring education and medical care, etc.? What could we add to our current portfolio that has the potential for the greatest impact?

Again, seek to add innovative initiatives, not to create a binary, either-or result where something is cut in favor of a new idea. Instead see them as building blocks over time that naturally help facilitate the growth of the project as things progress, grow, and expand. Someone may suggest doing more in the local sponsoring community as well. The appropriate response would be, "Great. Let's do that, too!" God desires us to be inspired to seek godly solutions to what often appear to be intractable problems, through creative, life-changing solutions involving the very people that they are designed to help as designers and implementers.

"THAT IS NOT HOW WE DO THINGS HERE"

Some people will inform you of the historical and cultural patterns of funding necessity that are now deemed the true mission expression of the organization, church, or ministry. Great! That is the solid foundation on which we are building in this new season as we partner with what God is doing.

Showing how the new model aligns with the history and previous mission partners helps support long-standing values, creating continuity with the past as you move into the future. This model is much more relationship intensive and local-expertise intensive than merely sending money to a charity or mission organization. Likewise, its fruitfulness is multiplied many times over as the Holy Spirit leads people to participate and share their talents, encouragements, and prayers with partners they know and are involved with. Over time, one will discover how God has specifically prepare them to be part of this and encourage this relational mission model by things they have learned in their respective journeys.

Essential Element VIII

Local Mission-Supporting Businesses and Income Types

35

Business Types, Sizes, and Levels of Economic Business Engagement

THERE ARE DIFFERENT TYPES and sizes of businesses that we will consider:

1. Sole proprietor.
2. Small business.
3. Medium-size business.
4. Large business.
5. Corporation.
6. Multinational.

When creating businesses whose profits will fund NGOs, nonprofits, and mission objectives for schools, seminaries, clinics, hospitals, and so on, the goal is twofold:

1. To create new businesses whose profits will fund the local charitable endeavors designed to change the community.
2. To stimulate the expansion of new businesses in the community by leveraging. . .

    a. *Economic diversification* through establishing medium-size businesses that pay higher wages and thereby produce higher incomes, which lead to the establishment of more small businesses to provide specialized services to the new higher wage earners.

b. *The introduction of new methods* and means related to agriculture, food production, or other local commerce.

ECONOMIC DIVERSIFICATION THROUGH MEDIUM-SIZE BUSINESSES

The creation of medium-size businesses, which employ six to eight employees or more, provides new options for employment. These businesses traditionally have a higher wage, which immediately affects the conditions of the family of a person working for one of the new businesses as well as those around them. These new employees will need housing, a new door, or perhaps a small room added to an existing structure; all of this creates opportunities for additional work in the village. This is the kind of economic expansion that traditional aid programs never touch and thereby are unable to make long-term economic and expansive change in a community.

UNDERSTANDING EXISTING CONDITIONS

Plot Farms

Poor rural communities tend to have small plot farms that serve a small family unit as a "subsistence farm." Every family will have and tend a plot of land that is usually no more than twenty feet by twenty feet, or thirty-seven square meters. Tilling, planting, weeding, and tending these garden plots takes up part of every day in the growing season. For many this follows the rainy season. Unfortunately, the plot farms only produce enough food for about nine months on average, not enough for a full year. This leads to the famine season.

One of our student leaders once asked a church member when the famine season was in Los Angeles. He was surprised to learn that there is no regular famine season in Southern California.

Work on the Plot Farm

All the work is done by hand, and the plot of land may be a walk of a mile or more from the village where they live. If conditions are dry that year, they will need to haul water as well by carrying it on their heads to supplement the moisture in the soil for the crops until rain comes. So, agriculture is one of our areas of new business enterprises and creative ventures in rural villages that we want to engage through various businesses and improved practices for yield and income. The size and impact of these businesses will vary.

DEFINING THE BUSINESSES

As stated above, there are different types and sizes of businesses, which we will define in a bit more detail.

1. *Sole Proprietor* (one-person shop): This type of business will affect the individual running the business and may provide increased income compared to merely tending the plot farm. Even so, opportunities are relatively limited within the village because it lacks resources to pay the sole proprietor for his or her services when the average living is only a dollar or two a day. (Ironically, most aid organizations focus their resources here.)

2. *Small Business* (one to two employees, not dominant in the industry, independent owners): These have an added benefit for the village over a sole proprietor in that skills are being passed along, usually to a younger (family member) apprentice, who also provides more physical labor to support the business. In this way a business and the essential skill set thereof are not lost to the village due to natural aging and attrition.

3. *Medium-Size Business* (six to eight employees): These businesses are our sweet spot because they do not require the capital needed for a large business, they are expandable, and they bring a higher wage to all their employees—providing an economic stimulus to the village. Another benefit is that, unlike large businesses, they do not draw the attention of corrupt governments seeking bribes.

4. *Large Businesses* tend to be in urban areas, and their only interaction with outlying areas is to purchase raw materials from the poor

villages, as in the case of cacao for making chocolate, or the mining of minerals, etc.

5. *Corporations* have a role to play in economic development, but their role is complex, as they are distant from the village. The primary concern is overall profit, which often conflicts with paying a reasonable price for the goods and materials that are purchased through intermediaries and consortiums from villages. The "bottom line" results in far less than a reasonable rate to secure fair wages or value for local products that could otherwise bring about local economic expansion.

6. *Multinationals* are similar to the above and have almost zero knowledge of the living conditions and cultures of the people with whom they are working indirectly in the supply chain. Whether dealing with rubber or cocoa, the local producer sells it to a middleman or consortium that "verifies" fair wages are paid and humane working conditions are upheld. These intermediaries in turn pay bribes to the local government officials, who provide cover and continue to take ancestral lands from villages to increase production for exportation of the cash crop. The multinationals are blocked by government officials from viewing the conditions of the local producers, and likewise they lack the cultural expertise to successfully make advancements, being ignorant of effective ways of changing local power structures to benefit the workers—instead of corrupt governments officials and the "cooperatives" they are in bed with. Additionally, there are local mafias cooperating with governments that will intervene to exploit their own people and harness the assets of the multinationals for their own benefit, at the expense of those who do the work.

Types 1–3

Our model focuses on the first three business types, as those are where local businesses can start with modest seed capital and then expand. These have the highest likelihood of success and tend to largely avoid the complexities and scale of corruptions that are an endemic part of the last three. Finally, small businesses are responsible for 80 percent of the jobs in the world, and although multinationals have huge resources, they are slow to adapt to new realities and regularly lay off employees in a downturn to preserve their profits and stock values.

HIGHEST RETURN

Entering global markets is the opportunity to make significantly more profit and to be paid in Western currencies that can be used to purchase computers and other Western goods, which are usually too expensive to purchase because of exchange rates and currency values. Multinationals are by nature players in the global markets and control much of the trade.

Finding opportunities closer to the consumer and in more affluent markets will bolster a business's income and future prospects for income; however, these are much more difficult to enter and maneuver in, and they should be considered in this light. Beginning in a local market and expanding toward a nearby city and then toward export is also a stepped strategy that allows for immediate income and expansion. It also allows for growth of the business, so growth parameters and benchmarks can be established for future expansion.

Export to foreign markets means interacting with more parties from the government and government entities, as well as navigating trade laws, cooperatives, and cartels. Each of these may exact a payment or cost that makes export difficult, if not impossible. Strategizing in consideration of all the above factors will help to ensure the wisest course of action available.

36

Socialism's Use of Social Justice to Exploit the Poor

DISCLAIMER FOR SOCIAL JUSTICE WARRIORS

SOME WHO ARE READING this may be inspired to take on the injustice of the last three business types (large businesses, corporations, and multi-nationals), and you may be disappointed about the lack of coverage in this book. We reiterate our focus on starting medium-size businesses for local markets as the most expeditious ways (if not the most profitable) of empowering people to fund hospitals, schools, clinics, and so forth. While becoming aware of the injustices that exist, there may be an impulse to seek justice and bring about fairer practices at the market for those selling their goods. If that is your passion, go for it. This is an extensive political process, both in the country of origin as well as the international maritime and transport laws and systems in the global shipping and distribution networks. That particular emphasis falls outside the scope of this work.

Our primary focus is on empowering people in ways that are effective and proven to work in a variety of countries, having borne fruit in a relatively short amount of time. Through these processes and ventures, the lives of families and whole communities are being transformed. Likewise, as wages increase through these practices, they put pressure on wages upward. Thus, through the markets, a challenge is presented to the corrupt alliances between governments and large businesses, which join together in exploiting laborers. When transformative steps are being taken, the people will now have other viable options, so the pressures of the market become part of the reforming structure for long-term change.

Is it enough? Economic empowerment is the best place to begin, but as with all things, it has its limitations. Even so, it is still the best and essential starting place to provide a foundational functionalism that moves the poor from their current state of fragility to greater economic empowerment.

HERE'S WHY IT IS DIFFICULT

Pseudo-government reform, multilayered systems of corruption, and bribes—which perpetually accompany the work of the deep pockets of multinational corporations and large NGOs working with corrupt governments—are a spider web of intricacies and cross-connections that seem to morph almost daily. As laws are changed, those with corrupt, exploitative agendas simply pivot or backflip to the next loophole that they can invent, weaving between the lines of existing laws in various jurisdictions, countries, and conditions. These problems are much more intractable and economically debilitating than they appear at first glance. They relate to the core of political greed born out of poverty and nurtured by the socialist governments whose excessive economic participation guarantees ready access to every facet of society, wherein they may operate their corrupt plans and schemes. Ultimately, this leads to the exploitation of peoples, resources, and lands by any and all who aspire to power—as their birthright of economic fratricide.

The system exists to promote the culture of bribery, corruption, payments, and extortions as their primary function; all others are secondary. Further complicating this, once one has entered the world of global supply chains, this "business of corruption" is inexorably drawn to the new economic activity, thereby attracting once again the worst elements of the web of corruption, bribes, and extortion that suck the lifeblood out of the economies that they should be protecting.

Ironically, these very governments are formed by more and more socialist agenda groups using the current exploitation of the people as grounds for being the new ones in power. They promise that the governments they form will write new constitutions and form new structures to provide even greater control over the society and economy so that everyone participates at an equal level. The first part is regularly executed; laws are written and the government takes an even larger part of the economy and essential services, giving them an even larger platform for corruption. But the economies they preside over wither away even more than before, and the corruption grows exponentially, requiring a new generation to hear the promises for the first time and to once again empower an elite class whose structures dominate the entire life of the society, education, healthcare, transportation, ports, resources, and economy. This agenda kills the creativity of the populace through control and command economies, and it further limits their ability to ever leave the permanent and growing lower class that these systems entrench and grow over time.

REFORM

These corruption challenges require long-term, systemic changes through legislation, legal enforcement (against the extortionist governments, officials, and local mafias), and global awareness to bring ongoing pressure promoting transparency and alleviating the exploitation of our brothers and sisters globally. More importantly, it will require prayer and fasting by the local churches to humbly seek God's face, to repent of the activity and their participation in it, and to seek a transformational change of heart. It is this heart change that will catalyze a lasting, robust change of practice that only God can bring through the working of his Spirit.

Example: Cocoa Farmers

As an example, the average cocoa farmer receives the equivalent of less than one penny per dollar of chocolate sold to the consumer. Would most people be willing to pay a penny more, doubling the income of the farmer? Is $1.01 for a chocolate bar a cost we are willing to bear so a farmer can pay school fees for his children? For most people, they will buy the $1.00 bar because it is cheaper, then send $40 a month to a charity to pay for the farmers child to go to school. Such is the world we live in.

Justice

It is far more just to pay the extra penny for the chocolate so that the farmer can benefit proportionally from his crop, care for his family, and expand his business in a self-sufficient way. This is preferable and brings more dignity and productivity than being humiliated by an unjust cartel with a controlled price, having your labor and investment devalued unfairly by this artificially low price for your product. This low price—created by greedy governments and officials, corrupt cooperatives, and complicit chocolate companies and their subsidiaries—perpetuates a modern-day share-cropping scam. All the while the farmer is living in fear that any protest could result in those with power taking vengeance. He fears they may burn his farm if he disrupts the system, fails to pay his bribes, or worse yet, interferes with the systems of corruption on which the mafias, governments, and multinationals dance about, either willingly or unwillingly, to do their dirty business.

GLOBAL CORRUPTION

The levels of duplicitous global corruption at play here are nearly impossible to fathom. Many nations of the European Union continue to have sovereignty over major ports in the developing world and magistrate these ongoing corruptions as a matter of policy to prop up their own economic interests. France controls the major port of Duala in Cameroon; no one can ship cocoa out of the port other than the cartels that supply the major chocolate producers. If one attempts to export cocoa outside of the cartel and they are discovered, the cocoa is destroyed, and the cartel permanently bans the grower from selling their cocoa in the future.

The wonderful people leading the European Union colossus of government in Belgium coincidentally sit in the same location where some of the largest global chocolate manufacturers are located. With one hand they set up commissions of highly paid government experts to investigate corruption in the global cocoa trade, producing lengthy reports and spending millions. With the other hand they increase production in the humming factories down the street, while the unseen cocoa farmers live in mud houses, drinking dirty water and are unable to afford school fees, medicines, and proper food for their children.

Cash Crop Value

Nonetheless, selling cocoa, even at the low price paid to the farmer, still has economic advantages over other locally consumed crops and remains a cash crop that brings increased benefits to the producers and their family. This is in spite of the fact that it is clearly not related to a fair living wage or a fair, open-market price.

Companies Paying Bonuses to Farmers?

Recently, Nestlé and others promoted on their websites how they are paying bonuses to the farmers through their intermediary buyers. I asked my cocoa-producing friends if they have seen any of that money. They laughed out loud and said the money will *never* come to the farmer. Without independent and competitive buyers, farmer-controlled cooperatives, free access to the ports, and freedom to export to any buyer without interference and government bribes, this will remain a system of exploitation.

It is ironic that the social justice warriors naively believe and advocate for solutions to this corruption through the very governments and the businesses that are involved in creating and maintaining the injustices that serve them. Moreover, it is inconceivably foolish that the perpetrators of corruption will become the source of solutions to the very corruptions that they create and maintain. How will these socialist governments—with absolute, expansive economic participation and control in these nefarious behaviors and practices—be expected to birth the reforms that stop lining their bribe-filled pockets and miraculously birth just legislation and enforcement from the bed of corruption itself? How long will it take for the exploiters to create the new systems of accountability, fairness, and transparency to take root and be implemented through the exploiters reforming themselves?

The social justice warriors will greatly increase in efficacious outcomes as they learn the value of open and fair markets in snuffing out unfair practices through competition and free trade. These are friends, not enemies. Social justice is not brought about by consolidating influence and economic power but by democratizing it and creating societies of law—not political and economic favorites.

Essential Element IX

Economic Expansion

Solutions or Supplements—The Need
for Capital Loans and Investment

37

Economic Empowerment

ECONOMIC EMPOWERMENT CAN HAPPEN. Here is how it can be done.

RAISING CAPITAL FOR NEW BUSINESSES

As we have seen, medium-size businesses play a crucial role in stimulating economic diversification, which promotes the creation of smaller businesses and sole proprietorships. A second step in the goal to lift communities from poverty-bound subsistence models—so that the subsistence culture can be moved off its stagnation point and expand more effectively—is tied to the need for additional capital and capital equipment as well as business knowledge and acumen.

Capital For Small Businesses

Economic diversification can bring about sufficient expansion of the local economy. A brick layer can purchase a trowel and bucket to begin his business, whereas a seamstress would need more capital to purchase a sewing machine and potentially a solar panel and inverter, so that her work would not be interrupted by the power outages that are so common in the developing world.

COMMUNITY BANK AND MICRO FINANCE

In the process of facilitating economic diversification, money to purchase tools and equipment to start small businesses and sole proprietorships can be provided by a *community bank*. Led by local investors, these banks, which will result from this new economic situation, can be used to provide access to capital that will be an outgrowth of the higher wages from those employed in the medium-size businesses. Powered by the increased wages and savings of these higher-wage earners, peer-to-peer borrowing and a community bank making small loans will undergird this expanding economic model. Implementing this as part of the local development plan, a local cooperative bank run by its investors can be an effective way of providing loans for capital materials or tools that are necessary to begin these small businesses or to expand them.

This is already a common practice and continues to expand globally, but the banks themselves do not produce the rate of return or create the economic diversification of medium-size businesses. They are a participatory structural piece in an overt economic enhancement but not a direct path to medium-size businesses with their higher wages and multiple employees. Sole proprietorships in the developing world tend to stay the way they start, as low-wage alternatives to other local employment. Only a very few will ever hire any additional labor, and usually it will be family.

NEXT PHASE

The capital required to fund an expansion to a medium-size business will most often require a larger asset base than what the local village can initially provide through its small investments and microloans. A larger asset base will be required. It is desirable to have all these options available, but it is not critical for all projects to commence. It is, however, important to see what resources are available and can be secured, perhaps through joining another cooperative community bank nearby. That said, waiting for a perfect system that has capital available for all contingencies will potentially cause unnecessary delay and complication, and the project may not begin at all while waiting for everything to be in place.

Community Banks and Microloans

Others have written on this and posted models online that give a more extensively thought through and thorough system for achieving, organizing, and structuring a community bank of this sort. There are a variety of different models, some of which have grown over time to have billions of dollars in loanable assets. One in India exclusively makes loans to women, some specialize in agriculture, and others create new opportunities outside of the agricultural economies that are the primary occupations of most rural villages. Although some villages are occupied by other industries or occupations (like fishing, mining, and tourism), there may be a way to innovate or expand into a new part of the business that could bring increased revenue to the village and higher-paying employment. In this circumstance, the community bank can focus on new endeavors by expanding beyond current opportunities or dominant employers in a particular sector.

This is why having local leaders who have traveled outside of the local context can be such a great asset, as they have been exposed to different types of services and activities that can be introduced locally and may boost commerce in regions beyond.

Each community is unique, and each of these banking models has advantages and disadvantages in size and type of loan, repayment schedules, available capital, mandatory investing rules for participants, and so on. Good advantage should be taken in seeking the wisdom of those operating in this field and inquiring how specific practices may apply to your local context as the community bank begins and expands over time. Explore loan limits, types of loans made, the purpose or structure of these loans, and if they achieve the long-term goals for the community.

Missing: Loans for Medium-Size Businesses

Finally, it is the larger loans (i.e., $50,000–$100,000 and up) required to expand growing businesses into the medium-size and larger business categories that require significant capital for equipment, tools, and land. These loans are rarely available in the developing world on reasonable terms for repayment and interest rates. Most require repayment within six months or less, and the interest rate can exceed 20 percent. This is too short of a cycle to install new equipment, let alone amortize the expense and produce adequate revenue to repay the entire loan.

PURCHASING LAND

The land must be purchased to avoid another kind of corruption. When a landlord sees that a tenant business is doing well financially or that the business owner or ministry has wealthy backers from abroad, it is common for the landowner to give short notice of a large rent increase—of 100 percent or more—due within one or two days. If the money is not paid, the landowner locks up the building and all the assets of the business, and claims they are in forfeiture for nonpayment of rent.

A Case Study

In Los Angeles is a prolific funder of church planting and founding mission organizations, schools, and clinics. Over time they developed a policy not to purchase land or build buildings due to the high rate of failures that this practice was producing. Ironically, the weakness in the plan was a lack of a coherent business model for running the new hospital or school that had local, long-term sources of income. With an enthusiastic visionary but no effective business model—with realistic income and expense projections and no proof of concept—failures were bound to occur. Because of these failures, they implemented a policy to not purchase land or build buildings. The problem with the model, however, was building too big, too fast and creating a heavy maintenance and operational burden before working out viable and ongoing cashflow for the ministry.

Many times this situation is created by the visionary leaders themselves. They believe that once the facility is completed, the church, having invested in the building, will naturally be obligated to preserve their honor and the initial significant investment, and thus keep supporting the work in perpetuity—even though that was not the original plan.

The entrepreneurial spirit of this church in pioneering new works globally is impressive. They have a specific group of people who review requests and make decisions on whether or not to fund them based on the merits of the ministry plan. The policy of not purchasing land directly, though, does jeopardize many of these ventures located on rental land as they grow and gain traction and become fruitful. These projects are subject to exploitation by greedy landlords making dramatic increases in rent and practicing this confiscatory theft, which does not have local legal protections and is quite common in the developing world.

Likewise, initially funding a large building and land project with no effective business model for operations or a sustainable income stream to pay staff is equally fraught with unnecessary and dangerous risks for the investment, causing the venture to fail. We have found a "proof of concept" phase and smaller-scale starting point to determine both the efficacy of the proposed plan and the community adopting the ministry, as well as the local leaders' ability to manage it in a healthy way, to be effective in avoiding both of these extremes. *Subsequently* purchasing a piece of land allows freedom to advance with flexibility, autonomy, and responsibility.

This approach takes longer and sometimes requires more involvement by the funding organization in the process, but the long-term fruitfulness and success of the ministry increase exponentially. However, if a sponsoring organization or church believes in the "go big or go home" model—and is willing to take on an assigned risk of larger ventures and a higher rate of failing as a percentage of those they sponsor—then that model may be preferable to them, although not advised here. Every organization planted as well as every sponsor has its own culture, personality, and uniqueness; they are not all alike.

Proof-of-concept models in the developing world can be rather slummy looking and feel beneath the status of the sponsoring organization. But it is not about them. Therefore, this requires reeducation of the sponsoring organization and its supporters, who often want to see new, beautiful, Western-standard facilities at every phase instead of a modest, one-room clinic progressively becoming a modern hospital over time.

38

The Crisis Trap

UNSPOKEN ASSUMPTIONS

A BOARD MEMBER I serve with told me of a partner whom he has sponsored for many years and who decided to expand the ministry work they were doing. The work required thousands of dollars, and they mentioned it to the sponsor as something they were pursuing. He told them that he would *pray* for them and the new venture. They came back to him later saying they desperately and urgently needed his support for the expanded venture, and without it they would fail and lose what had already been invested. They pleaded with him based on the prior relationship and pending need and crisis. My friend did not have the resource to finish this project for them, let alone fund the obligations for the ongoing operational expenses as they desired.

DANGEROUS ASSUMPTIONS AND PRESUMPTIONS

Many from the developing world make assumptions based on their own beliefs, values, practices, or understandings of how others will likely behave. The *crisis method* is commonly used to create or use an impending disaster to make an *urgent* request for the sponsor to *rescue* their friend from trouble. As an example, in most African cultures, it is a common assumption and cultural expectation that when there is an emergency, everyone in the village and clan will chip in resources to help in the crisis. Participation is expected to be given in proportion to the person's wealth, assets, and abilities. This same local assumption can spread over the globe to their new honorary friend or citizen of the village who has sponsored a prior project. Therefore, if there is a crisis, they are cordially obligated to participate in funding the solution through an urgent donation proportionate to their wealth. Since they are very wealthy by global standards and the project is of such great merit, a significant donation is inevitable and mandatory in the face of a looming crisis.

From a Western cultural perspective, this is a gross imposition without a proper request of funds or any kind of plan that they have reviewed in advance to specifically participate in. Many in the majority world believe the following about those in the West: first, they have nearly unlimited potential to give; second, Westerners regularly respond charitably to global disasters; third, they will respond favorably in the same way that a local would be compelled to respond to the crises-culture obligation—after all, they now view this Western partner as "one of them" and have told them so repeatedly as a compliment. This is further exacerbated by the "well of blessing" belief. According to this belief, the local poor need access to the "well of blessing," and once they find it, they will be blessed and can draw freely from it. Once the well is discovered, no other wells are searched for because there are few (if any) wells available in one's lifetime; therefore, one ought not be greedy for other wells and should simply exploit the one at hand.

These are all false assumptions and can create relationship-ending tensions and consequences, which were never anticipated by those requesting the funds and make little sense to them based on their worldview. From a Western perspective, a fraud has been perpetrated by forcing the donor into fulfilling an urgent commitment that they did not make or assent to, all without their permission. Meanwhile, the locals perceive the past and ongoing support of their project as a cultural commitment to be "with them" through good times as well as hard times, further obligating them to "help out" in the future according to their relative financial ability, which is perceived as being significant, if not limitless. And if they are limited, certainly someone from their local tribe also has unlimited resources and could easily be asked to help with this urgent crisis in an obligatory manner, as is common in their culture. *Or not. . .*

DANGERS OF LONG-TERM SUBSIDY AND SUPPORT

Unfortunately, this common, ongoing-subsidy-funding model creates an endemic dependency that undermines local income production and the ministry's long-term ability to functionally thrive and grow. However, when using the local, new-business-profits funding model, many of these assumptions can be avoided just by the function of the model itself, which fosters independence and local accountability. No profit, no money. Beyond donation or loanable assets for initially establishing ministries, any future expansion at each level of this model will be funded by local projects and businesses created and managed by the local leaders. These leaders will be informed that their ability to succeed is paramount, as there will be no monthly stipends or crisis donations to fund this work in the future; they are responsible for its success or failure, so they must choose well.

The Western partner will be available for counsel and prayer only—but not to bail them out with financial resources. New projects in new communities are on the horizon. Projects that cannot self-manage their resources are a liability and may require liquidation or donation to another entity that can manage them appropriately. *Give the talent to the one who has the most.* Sink or swim, as is said in the West. The project now has the resources to succeed both in ministry and income. We believe in you and your leadership, and we are looking forward to your success and what you will be able to teach others through your experience as you grow. Without building a relationship with the key leader(s) in a Western context, it is difficult for the locals in the village to understand these cultural differences, and it requires someone with experience to regularly explain the reality of the situation and the relationship.

When we create a dependency on ourselves in relation to a person or group of people in another country or community, we are inadvertently placing ourselves in the savior's role and unintentionally stunting their growth. It is tempting to be the "noble rescuer" in a crisis, or to likewise give someone the honor of being the "great benefactor," but both of these undermine the long-term success of the local leaders and their empowerment toward sustainability and growth.

39

Creating Resiliency with
No Dependency

ROBUST SUSTAINABILITY

WHEN REBEL GROUPS STARTED forming in Cameroon to overthrow the president, the government shut down their banana plantations, which are located in the jungles where they rebels were hiding. Twenty-six thousand poor plantations workers lost their employment. One of our partners told me of the local plight of those on the plantation and how he had set a up a class to teach these displaced workers how to start their own small businesses. All he needed was the capital to seed the businesses, about $700. My first Western impulse was to find and send him the money. But we refrained and instead prayed. A few days later he told me they had sold one of the pigs from the pig farm. We helped start with seed capital, and the money from the sale of the pig would cover the expenses of seeding the new business ventures and would be paid back with a small interest by those receiving the funds.

Small-Scale Loans

What I learned from my partner is that they took what would normally be a profit item to them to operate the other charities (the money from the sale of the pig) and converted it into a loanable asset to be repaid as a group of short-term interest-bearing loans to the budding entrepreneurs. This was a genius solution that would not exist for future practice, benefit, and expansion of ministry and economic resources if the Western urge to be "the savior in all things" had prevailed. Now, we can both bless others in their creativity and engagement by utilizing this creative solution well into the future. The profit from the pig was multiplied by the interest earned from the loans to the new entrepreneurs, a local win and an economic enhancement as resources continue to move, grow, and expand locally.

Kiva, Heifer International, and others

Kiva is the brainchild of a Stanford University graduate. This nonprofit offers small loans through local agents that are crowdfunded online in the United States through its website. These small loans are then repaid to the lender in the U.S. on a set schedule; they have a low default rate compared to much of the developing world, which can be as high as 70 percent.

Heifer International donates cows, water buffalo, alpacas, chickens, and honeybees to promote economic growth in rural villages. They also provide training in how to manage and maintain the livestock through their program. The goal is to lessen poverty through locally sustainable productivity by introducing livestock animals on a small scale and new practices like honeybees.

The goal for all of these is reducing poverty instead of building wealth. But are they not the same thing? No. Reducing poverty is a noble idea and will reduce the suffering of the poor, but it is not the same as focusing on building wealth in a community. Building wealth focuses on expansion and multiplication, including practices like large herd grazing as biomimicry, being promoted by Janine Benyus in her six books on the topic. Allan Savory has written books in a similar vein, including the *Holistic Management Handbook,* and his 2013 TED Talk on desertification—with over 8.8 million views—argues for more expansive herds to reclaim lands from desertification while increasing crop yields and mitigating carbon in the atmosphere.[1] Large herds move and fertilize as they eat and trample down dead grasses to make way for the new ones in the springs; with their cloven hooves turning the soil, they naturally produce

---

1. Savory, "How to fight desertification."

fertilizer to join with the seeds for next year's grasses. The waste from the animals prevents over-grazing. Conversely, lone animals or small herds eat everything green and cause harm to the environment.

Watch the herds crossing the savannah. They number in the thousands, as did the buffalo on the North American continent. God makes big herds and blesses us in big ways. When Abraham was blessed, it was not with one cow, sheep, or camel but thousands (see Genesis 13:1–6.).

CAPITAL EQUIPMENT TO EXPAND AND MECHANIZE MEDIUM-SIZE BUSINESSES

Coffee Plantation in Nigeria

A young entrepreneur in Nigeria wanted to start a local coffee brand and small coffee shops to raise capital to assist young women in Abuja, many of whom moved there for education but often found themselves renting rooms for stay that turned into demands by the landlord for sexual favors. This common plight often left these girls vulnerable, lost, and without the resources to extricate themselves from this plight. They were threatened with the removal of all their possessions if they could not pay the rent immediately. This would place them on the streets, even more vulnerable to forms of extreme manipulation and exploitation.

In the process of setting up the first coffee store, our entrepreneur came in contact with a family that now controlled a former large-scale, colonial coffee farm. The new owners, however, did not have a background handling a coffee business of this scale. They dried the beans on cloths laid on the ground and roasted them in small, clay pots over an open fire. They did not have experience that utilized modern equipment suitable to the scale of the large coffee farm's production that was now under their management. Likewise, they did not have the resources or expertise to acquire the necessary equipment to process the harvest, package it, or do the sales and marketing necessary and get it to market successfully.

The unrealized potential of this coffee farm business is readily apparent. It could employ many people and sell its crop for thousands (if not more) on the global market, depending on whether they sold a consumer-ready product or sold their crop in bulk to a distributor, or both. All of this also depends on effective management. Even in this situation, many who purport to help, particularly from the West, may not be trusted because a smart partner may make them indebted with expensive equipment that they cannot afford and do not understand how to effectively run and maintain. The loan to buy such equipment creates a liability, which encumbers their property and is then used to cheat this family out of their business and its profits to repay the debt—leaving them poorer than before. There are so many ways this could go right or terribly wrong, particularly in a place that is known for its corruption.

This is not a $50 (Kiva) loan solution. Indeed, it would be beyond a microloan banking situation, either locally managed or through an international partner. The burden of a high-interest, short-term loan is also a risk that could see this potentially profitable opportunity fall from the family's grasp and leave them without the business, poor and in debt. Whom can they trust as a partner? Who can help them?

Oranges in Malawi

In a Malawian village about forty-five minutes from the city is an area that grows maize (corn), and the region is also replete with oranges. When the oranges are ripe, the locals celebrate and start eating oranges. After a while, they have had their fill, and many oranges fall to the ground and rot. There is no way to get them to the markets in the nearby city; they do not have the containers to transport them in bulk, let alone in packages that can be used in a local market. The roads are poor, and fruit falling off a truck is common. Additionally, the large ruts and potholes compress the fruit, further damaging the crop and reducing the amount that can be sold. Likewise, the value of the crop in this type of situation is already fairly low when everyone else has ripe fruit to be sold at the same time.

Potential solutions would be to harvest the fruit in store-ready containers or shipping boxes. A third option is using storage containers that could be kept in a cool house suspending the ripening process and then bringing the fruit to market when the competition had sold out. This would require local transport from the fields to a refrigerated cool house, protective transport packaging for storage materials, and transport to the markets in the city. Each of these stages and phases would provide local employment and opportunities for a small transport business as well as workers to harvest fruit that would otherwise rot on the ground.

From a global perspective, the crated fruit could be put in refrigerated shipping containers, and it could travel to Europe or other parts of the continent for sale, as well as Israel and the Middle East.

GLOBAL MARKETS: SUPPLY CHAIN EXPERTISE

Places we have mentioned like Malawi, Nigeria, and other nations do not lack in natural resources. They simply need partnerships to harness and grow the resources they already have that are underproducing; thereby they can expand the market potential as they become more productive in a functional supply chain. This requires business expertise, not aid workers handing out bags of rice or paying school fees. More than handouts, people want to have an opportunity to be productive and bless their family and community.

Entering global markets can be one of the most challenging and lucrative options, but it has its challenges to go along with the opportunity.

All of us can be part of that. The pathway is strategic and relational. It requires an investment of thought, prayer, planning, and knowing and loving people. It leads to celebrating the success that they experience as they overcome new hurdles and live out the use of their gifts, talents, and resources for the glory of God.

Creating structures that lead to wealth building for families and communities is the goal, rather than alleviating just some of the symptoms of poverty. When the Bible says that God blessed Abraham (see Genesis 13:2 and 24:25), it lists extensive livestock that he had, which numbered over a thousand. God's ways have not changed, and although not everyone will attain the same level of abundance as Abraham, we operate in a God-created world of abundance, not scarcity. The purveyors of socialism and communism regularly spew forth scarcity as part of a doctrine of living subjugated under the authority of an elite power class for the common good. This type of thinking consistently leads to tyranny wasting the multiplying talents of creative innovators while trapping the majority of people within the lower of two classes—the ruling elite and the poor—with no mobility upwards. This is the utopian cell in the new order offered by those promising so-called equality and equity.

Finally, we have learned that medium-size businesses and larger are required to move a local economy from subsistence to economic expansion and growth. Only then do we start to realize the different potentials of each person blessing the larger community, as they grow their gift's capacity through training and education, while creating and investing in opportunities of various sizes and scales. Medium-size businesses produce up to 80 percent of new jobs in expanding economies; they are, therefore, essential to the wellbeing of an economy and the thriving of a nation.

40

The Local Leadership Challenge

IN THE LAST CHAPTER we looked at the importance of medium-size businesses, management, and business growth. In this chapter we will explore the type of leader who can lead a board that manages multiple businesses and ministries.

The *manager of multi-site, multilocation ministries and businesses* should have several required characteristics. This leader is not an emperor with subjects to order around, nor simply a facilitator to amplify and cheerlead local success. Rather the manager is a leader of leaders who is still the boss, who can work with the board to expand enterprises, and who is responsible to hire and fire as necessary. This last part is generally done in cooperation with the board. "Hire slowly, fire quickly" is the saying, although most do the opposite, to their detriment. Church leaders in particular welcome readily and seek to retain and restore people instead of letting them move on when they have ceased to be a blessing—and are, in fact, causing great harm with increasing regularity. Retention in a particular situation is not to be confused with redemption, which may take a trip through the wilderness before the adequate character has been grown to enter the promised land with a newfound readiness to serve faithfully after this transformative experience.

BOARD LEADERSHIP

This leader has a board of talented leaders from the larger and surrounding community who are committed to the vision. Generally, the board members are not compensated; they have their own employment with expertise that assists the board in making decisions, and they are serving to make the community better through cooperation with and expansion of the ministry. They are not from a single church but from several, to increase the connections available and avoid control by any specific church, leader, or other group that might be a conflict of interest.

Board Members

The board members have varied areas of expertise and connections that are needed and related to the various businesses and ministries for which they will be responsible. They do not manage the day-to-day operations of any of the businesses or ministries, as the operations are delegated to hired managers, who are paid by the businesses and ministries that they lead. The board is responsible for the over-all functioning of all of these entities and will help to set, maintain, and achieve specific goals. The goals are to be clearly stated in writing and undergo review both annually and more frequently with each local manager.

The board members also function to replace the lead person or manager within each entity if their work is underperforming or there is a problem related to finances or the like. This function is performed as a part of their fiduciary responsibility for oversight.

Board Leader/Chair

The board is led by the ministry leader whose vision initially started the ministries or their successor. This person will have demonstrated the ability to be a leader of leaders and to envision and facilitate the growth of the ministries over time. They are also mentoring and influencing other leaders who are being developed to establish new ministry models in the communities they serve.

Not all visionary leaders have the capacity to lead other established and talented leaders; however, this level of skill is required to effectively grow to a point where medium-size businesses are being established.

Managing people is key for a medium-size business or organization. Leading well and managing well, and letting people go when they do not support the vision, are essential skills that must be possessed and continually developed. The board will also work with the board chair or president to make sure the necessary skills are developed that may need expansion in new areas, as the organization grows and becomes more diverse and complicated. The board leader does not receive primary compensation for their service and leadership on the board.

Wealth Builder: The Builder of People

This leader realizes that the most important resource they have is their people. They strive to support the managers in their work, anticipating struggles and together being prepared for challenges with solutions before they are needed. This type of person is essential on a board, and their activity is one of empowerment. It is not based on positional authority but empowering those with a title to affect the goals they are seeking to fulfill.

PREVENTING AND DEALING WITH INFRACTIONS

The board and its chair will together identify and set up systems of accountability that allow the organization to thrive. They create clarity and allow for a clear direction in the daily operation of the organization. However, if those standards are violated, action is quickly taken to bring the matter to the attention of the manager and to get a swift resolution of the problem. If the manager is unable to cooperate in the process, the board shall be notified that the manager's services are no longer required.

Critical Failure

This is the critical area where most people fail as leaders, particularly visionaries in ministries, by trying to give too many chances, too many times, to too many people. In doing so, they are creating a standardless culture of confusion and lawlessness, which ultimately breeds a culture of disrespect, reduces the morale of the best team players, and promotes the lethargy and indifference of the worst on the team. Over time it also leads to gossip, backbiting, complaining, and jealousies, as some who work harder than others begin to resent the fact that they're carrying other peoples' loads without compensation or appreciation. This kind of injustice is toxic to any ministry or business and must be expeditiously addressed.

In longer-standing organizations, a person may have long-term employment and therefore may have ingratiated themselves into the organization; they are perceived to be "essential" or too difficult to replace, based on the assumed fallout that will come. Again, in these circumstances, too many chances and a failure to positively address and provide a successful, guided, accountable pathway for successful change is regularly missing.

Question 1: How many bad employees does it take to ruin a ministry? Answer: *One*

Question 2: How many bad members does it take to ruin a church? Answer: *One*

Question 3: How many bad employees or leaders should you have? Answer: *None*

For most leaders, as they achieve leadership over multiple organizations, they will find this to be the area of greatest struggle, and this will need the highest level of encouragement from their board as they pursue excellence and effectiveness in all of the ministries for which they share in leadership responsibility. Many board members are tempted to let the leader stand alone when tough decisions have repercussions that bring about criticism. However, this also denotes those on the board who have the necessary skills to lead and those who are easily tempted to be exclusively liked and praised.

Loss of reputation, income, and ministry effectiveness are just some of the deficits that will have to be overcome when these challenges are not addressed in a timely manner. They can cost the organization significant funds and participation over a long period of time.

OTHER CHARACTERISTICS: FORWARD VISION

Staffing

This leader needs to have the ability to look forward many years. Forward vision needs to be part of their makeup so that they can see trends coming, identify where leaders and managers are advancing in their skills, or notice the decline in a leader's skills or influence that may warrant removal. To be effective as a leader is to be observing and anticipating these things, with plans in place for likely eventualities.

Resources

Likewise, they need to be looking at the future of the businesses and the ministries and anticipating what they are going to be needing. This activity runs parallel to consulting with the managers of the businesses and ministries, asking them what they anticipate they need right now, in the next six months, and in the next year or two. Keeping track of these needs and planning around them strategically—looking for opportunities and addressing these issues with the board and the relative budgets—will make the board and all of its entities highly functional.

Failure to do this work will result in doing a lot more problem solving and putting out fires that will inevitably come up because the future was not anticipated appropriately. Solving problems is more time and resource consuming than anticipating and planning for them, and it has much less drama.

Planning

The ability to work and plan for the future is often more of a talent initially, but it is a skill that can be learned. In either case it is an absolutely essential practice, and as part of the board, these planning processes will focus on paying attention to the future and listening to those closest to the work. These are the key talents and abilities of effective leaders. Hewlett-Packard called this MBWA: "management by wandering around." Many people will suffer in silence and keep solutions to themselves until asked.

There is usually an inverse relationship between those who are highly skilled as operational managers and those who are visionary leaders, who see into the future and pursue it passionately. It is important to realize when one has a skilled operational manager, as they are essential to the organization and its healthy growth, that they will regularly struggle when it comes to seeing trends in the future and how adaptations for what has not yet happened can be implemented effectively.

The manager's primary ability is in maintaining what is going on in an effective fashion. The visionary's primary skill is in reworking, rebuilding, and creatively innovating past obstructions and emerging difficulties to see things in a new light, adapting for a new season. These are their gifts, and they often operate in what appears to be a juxtaposition to the skills of the manager. Yet, they are complementary and simply allow an organization to move past the speed bumps that arise with certainty over time—to bring about a new, adapted system of functioning that the manager can effectively coordinate in the season ahead after it is refined and constructed.

HOW CAN YOU IDENTIFY A LEADER OF LEADERS?

In order to identify a leader of leaders in a given community, simply go for a walk with them in the community where they live. You will find as they are walking along that person after person will approach them to tell or ask them something. Their standing in the community is high and their opinion is sought after because it is profound, effective, and moves toward building peace.

How Not to Identify a Leader of Leaders

Believing that just because people who have particular titles, credentials, or academic degrees must then have the innate ability to lead other leaders is a mistake. These tend to be the standards that the world uses to assign or gain leadership positions of authority and power within organizations. However, having a leadership title within an organized structure can speak either of the person's ability and talents to lead others, or equally replaceable, of their prowess to move themselves forward through the creative work of political manipulation or creating an image for themselves. One cannot always tell by looking from the outside whether a person simply has authority over other leaders because of title or because of their influence and gifting.

In the New Testament the title was *apostle*; the apostles were the leaders of leaders. The Apostle Paul is an example of a leader who influenced the whole of the early church but was not one of the twelve who ministered with Jesus during his earthly ministry walking with him from village to village.

REPLACING A LEADER OF LEADERS

When the founding leader moves on to other things, or retires or needs to be replaced for some other reason, the board will encounter potential candidates who are passionate about the ministry and still others who see the opportunity as a stepping stone to other things that will bring them the stature they have longed to achieve—too often at the expense of the ministry itself. These are challenging differences in priorities that are difficult to easily discern and that complicate the process of selecting a new leader. Deliberate seasons of prayer and fasting are necessary to arrive at a decision based on "peace that passes all understanding" and can go beyond appearances of personality and competences.

God uses the foolish things to confound the wise. Human beings use credentials, experience, recommendations, physical appearance, charm, influence, and prestige as our standards. We want to take pride in securing the highest caliber person with the most impressive pedigree; thus emerges the temptation to choose for our own someone who is seeking their own will, which creates a perfect match of ineffectuality, drama, and distraction—usually culminating in separation and disappointment.

RECOMMENDATIONS

A highly recommended associate pastor was hired to help in a growing church. The recommendations even came from some of the closest friends of the senior pastor, from colleagues and past mentees. The associate came in and quickly worked to undermine the senior pastor, seeking to take his position. When the leadership took action to correct the behavior, the associate quickly took leave of the church but took multiple families with him to establish another church by speaking against the senior pastor and making false and misleading accusations.

Later interviewing one of the mentees who had recommended this person for the associate pastor position, I inquired as to why they had made the recommendation. The reply surprised me: "We thought he might do better in the U.S. than he had done here and that this would be a good opportunity for him to make a new start." That, of course, is not what was communicated when the recommendation was made.

Be careful to ask probing questions about someone's ability to work with others productively. Here are two examples: "How would you rate them on a scale of one to ten? Where do they thrive and where are they still growing?" The caution here is that even someone who is a highly prized and trusted friend may still make a recommendation that is not in the best interest of the organization you serve.

MINISTRY AND BUSINESS

The ideal leader needs a mixture of gifts in understanding how a ministry operates and how a business operates, as well as the differences between the two. These are not easy people to find; most often they have specific skills related to one area or the other but with little overlap. For most ministry organizations with a business, the leaders will tend to have more skills in the ministry area and less in the business area. This is confounded by the fact that those with the ministry gifts and expertise tend to view them as being superior to the mundane gifts of business affairs that fund the organizations and are crucial to the running of the ministry.

Rejecting Business-Learning Opportunities

On one occasion, while speaking to Fuller Seminary's retired business administrator of 28 years, he told me how they offered classes in administration tuition free at the seminary, and yet the students didn't sign up for them. Only after graduating did they realize the deficit they had without those skills.

Prayerless Planning

Moreover, a business and church leader once wisely told me, as I struggled to assist someone seeking a grant, that "ignorance and arrogance have never been mutually exclusive." Unfortunately, many who lack in the understanding of the skills of running the business part of any organization often view that work as not only inferior but will brush it off as something lesser that should not intrude on their grand visions and dreams. They believe that it will self-solve in the long run because they presume upon the Holy Spirit to intervene and take care of every part of their divinely inspired plans. The Holy Spirit is able to do amazing things, but we should not presume upon him by lacking in skills and understanding related to costs and consequences of our actions, and by being in constant need of miraculous interventions to countermand our ignorant incompetency and negligence. Prayer is the starting place; listening to God is the step-by-step guidance along the way, not the last-resort backstop for poor decision making (see Psalm 199:105).

In this context, the word that is guiding us is *rhema*, God's voice speaking to us about our situation through the Bible, people, circumstances, inner urgings, closed and open doors, etc. It is God's guiding word and direction for our life's decisions and path.

Essential Element X

Social Justice and Compassion: The Great Divide

Working Together to Invest in What Is Working

41

Keys to Transformation and Language

FACT: OVER THE LAST two decades, more people have been brought out of abject poverty globally than in the preceding one hundred years. That is good news, but a lot of work still needs to be done. The shared goal is eradicating poverty; the pathways and language are divergent, but the practice of sending aid as transfer payments is common either through charities or governments with the same poor results.

OUR LANGUAGE: JUSTICE VS. COMPASSION VS. CHARITY

For many years addressing the issues of poverty were referred to as *charity*. Later it took on the title of *compassion*. (Both are good, biblical words, by the way.) Of late we hear the word *justice*. In the evolution of these words, charity and compassion are viewed as weak words by the social justice crowd, having taken on the connotation of being an elective or optional activity, for people who chose to be involved if they feel like it. In light of the fact that the vast bulk of community development and donations take place under these rubrics, they are deemed inadequate and misleading.

```
                              POVERTY

          Righteous Anger                    Heartfelt
                                            Compassion

                          Aid Focused

     Politically Funded                      Church Funded

                           No Trust

     Leftist Policies                        Apolitical
        Aligned

                          Corruption

  Communist/Socialist                        Economic
                                            Exploitation
```

| JUSTICE | Solution: TRANSFER PAYMENTS | COMPASSION |

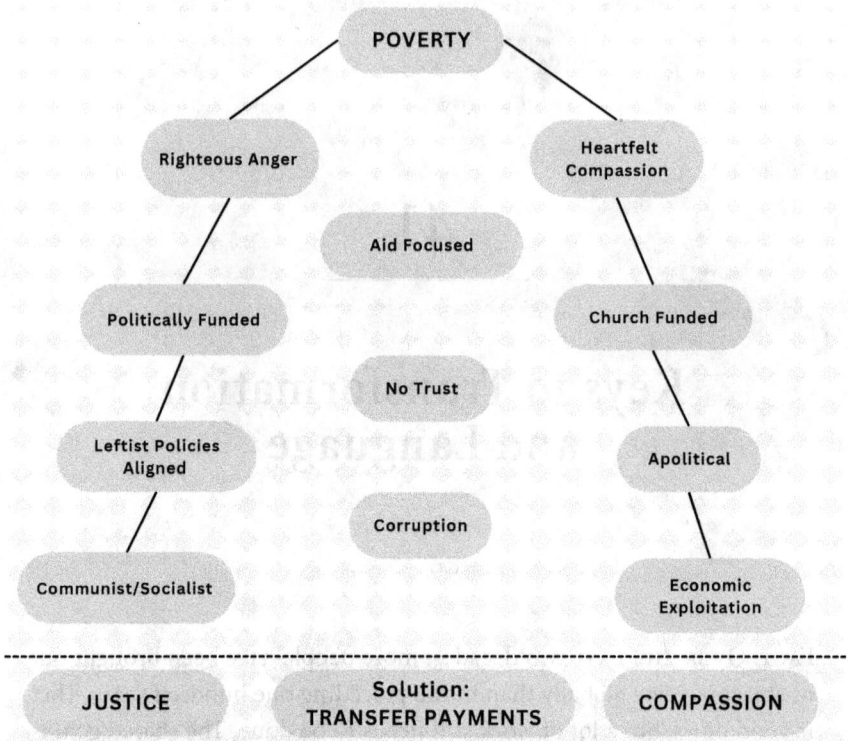

The social justice crowd has gone to great lengths to demonstrate, advocate for, and make the biblical case of necessity and mandate for of all of us to be involved and engaged in "justice issues," intentionally and actively fighting poverty—not as an elective matter but rather because the Bible simply demands justice. They disdain the view that addressing issues of the poor can take place as an act of common decency.

COMMON TACTICS: IRONY

The greatest irony as people squabble over terminology and relative levels of urgency is the common pathway that both groups engage in by using transfer payments to deliver aid. Social justice warriors tend to utilize governmental structures, the U.N., and others, whereas the compassion/charity folks will utilize NGOs, like Compassion International or World Vision. In both cases transfer payments are used to fund what is being done. Arguing over the relative size of the transfer payments and their relative pathway does not empower the poor to start businesses, increase their incomes, or change their circumstance; it simply leaves them stuck in their poverty, with the addition of a school or clinic, which in time will close for lack of funds.

"He has told you, O man, what is good; and what does the Lord require of you but to do justice, and to love kindness, and to walk humbly with your God?" (Micah 6:8).

ANGER INTRUSION

As justice has gained ascendancy in the larger society, it has tended to become in the seminary and church a legalistic, outward-focused mandate of compulsory involvement for the true followers of Jesus. This is in contrast of how it is described in the Old Testament as "naturally and continually rolling down like waters overflowing from lives well lived." Instead its proponents have sought to show its essential supremacy over things like corporate worship, and it has taken on an air of condescension, anger, and condemnation of anyone who does not subscribe to everything that any particular social justice warrior is advocating for on any specific topic.

This perspective toward action is justified by verses like Amos 5:23–24: "Take away from me the noise of your songs; to the melody of your harps I will not listen. But let justice roll down like waters, and righteousness like an ever-flowing stream." Instead of understanding these verses as describing true devotion and worship to God as having a consequent and practical outflowing (and not being simply confined to the place of corporate worship), they interpret that corporate worship is to be shunned if it does not favor and promulgate specific social action. This could result from a surface reading of this text, but the primacy of worship is a robust topic in the Bible. A more wholistic understanding is a lifestyle of worship where our weekly activity is in service to God, including when we gather together but not just limited to that.

JUSTICE OVER RELIGION

Amos clearly points out the divine preference for an outflow of the heart that results in justice and righteousness, as opposed to being isolated in the exclusive confinement of beautiful songs of worship that result in ecstatic emotion but do not result with an outward manifestation in the crucial issues of a whole life reflecting God's love.

The social justice crowd tends to subjugate personal righteousness as the proper manifestation of social justice alone, while accusing the compassion crowd of seeking personal righteousness and wrongly viewing justice as an optional, extracurricular activity. The compassion crowd believe that personal righteousness avoids all sorts of evil that contribute to poverty and oppression, and it is an essential characteristic of a person devoted to God, including corporate worship. They view the social justice crowd as adopting anger and animosity as legitimate bedfellows of personal righteousness properly enacted through justice—without any hint of personal righteousness in the individual's life. In fact, they view this anger and animosity as impediments and contrary to personal righteousness, not as pathways to social justice.

Likewise, the two parties are divided over political engagement. The social justice warrior group aligns with globalist, leftist, socialist policies and structures to force the world to address the issues of poverty through increased centralized authority for "fairness." They intend to use this as a means of bringing true justice through mandated transfer payments of wealth.

The compassion crowd rejects this statist model as a legitimate pathway, as it is tied to the creation of tyrannical socialist governance that destroys individual human rights and leads to anti-Christian governments, corrupt societies, exploitation of their people, waste of resources, and millions of needless casualties.

The social justice warriors counter that we must do something to combat this pervasive poverty and inequality, and in order to be effective, it must be mandated through legislation. Further, they will protest that they do not want in any way to promote totalitarian powers; merely they require the authority to wipe out inequity and poverty through mandated, organized policy making and economic reform, which they will control. They argue that true socialism and communism have never been implemented before, but they will bring about the true reform and the freedom that people long for.

INBORN JUSTICE

An experiment done on children under the age of 14 months showed them two small puppets interacting with one another. One of those puppets took a toy from the other puppet and hit the other puppet; they recorded the facial expressions of these small children and their reactions to the scenario. Their faces contorted in genuine anger and dislike toward the aggressive puppet that was stealing and hitting the other puppet. When given a chance to hold the puppets, the children chose to hold the puppet that had been abused and rejected the abuser.

It appears that something is built into us that has to do with justice, as well as our complete disdain toward those who directly misuse and abuse others. Scripture speaks of the inherent nature of human beings, apart from God's explicit commandments, in this way: "They show that the work of the law is written on their hearts, while their conscience also bears witness. . ." (Romans 2:15).

For many in the social justice crowd, they want to accuse anyone who has not joined with them in the totality of their endeavor and belief system of being complicit with, if not equal to, an abuser, and they use the tactics of shaming, guilt, and name calling to put that idea forward on a consistent basis in a rather haughty, self-righteous manner. Unfortunately, as a concept gains ascendancy in a group or larger part of society, it tends towards self-righteousness, which is repugnant to those outside the group and ultimately diminishes their cause. It replaces the critical thought, reflection, and refinement that are necessary in any growing endeavor to be successful and vital. Otherwise, these essential things are replaced with dutiful orthodoxy, politically correct speech, dutiful recitations, and blind following, which provides the perfect ground for coercive leadership to emerge and thrive while exploiting the faithful.

Dealing with some of the more intractable causal structures and entanglements that are key in perpetuating much of the poverty seen today is not easily engaged due to their complexity, as we have discussed in prior chapters. Yet, compassionate and loving people really do want to make a difference, but they really do not know what to do that will be effective. This sentiment toward compassion and justice is clearly indicated by the billions of dollars that are given by individuals, groups, and governments to change the plight of the poor, the oppressed, the refugee, or the internally displaced person. However, the solution of social justice warriors and the compassion crowd focuses almost exclusively on the failed systems of transfer payments from those with more to those with less. Overly simplistic, this approach does not empower people; instead it enslaves them to perpetual serfdom with their hands raised to their benefactors for one more handout. So, the solution to protest louder and add more righteous anger is not the pathway to our mutually shared goal.

We can do better. And we already are by empowering local leaders to transform their communities through establishing medium-size businesses, which support the families in the local community to build schools for their children, provide medical care through clinics and hospitals, raise up leaders of peace through the local churches planted, and reform agricultural practices to increase yields through sustainable practices that benefit the planet.

In the long run, depending on the emotion of anger is neither a unifier nor a long-term motivator toward a good direction. Untethered anger acts out against people both internally and externally, and it reacts to people in ways that cause harm, disunity, and damage to the very cause of the people whom we longed to help effectively.

CORE PERSPECTIVES

Social Justice Warrior

So, for the social justice warrior, participation on behalf of the poor is not optional. If someone thinks it is optional, they are duplicitous and evil according to this crowd and are a candidate for reeducation or doxing.

Compassion

For the compassion crowd, they value their freedom and do not need anyone interfering with it. They are accustomed to the organizations and pathways of sending aid to the developing world, and even though they do not change the overall circumstances, they prefer this to people losing more freedoms through leftist governments. And they will oppose perceived leftist agendas to address global problems out of hand. Likewise, the anger and vitriol demonstrated by others in their causes indicate a lack of necessary righteousness, and these people accordingly cannot be engaged effectively outside of their dysfunctional, divisive behaviors and must be politely avoided.

FORGIVENESS ENACTED

Since we have the same outcomes at heart—and ironically have perused the same principle of transfer payments, albeit through varying structures and agendas—let us take a moment to forgive each other and understand that all of us are weak and frail, functioning inside of systems that we did not create on our own but that we can be part of redeeming, to the glory of God. That redemption begins with forgiveness, because anything less will only bring new and more victims, here and abroad.

Forgiveness is a decision. It is a recollection and releasing. Forgiveness is a continued, intentional reality. It involves an expectation of a present and future reality unburdened by the past errors, mistakes, and offenses. Forgiveness is an essential part of the transformation of our world. We cannot get control back into our lives and our work when we focus exclusively on what went wrong or who did wrong, instead of pursuing positive transformation. We are people of accomplishment and forward movement, not people of complaint and blaming.

We must move forward.

42

The Legislation Trap

TACTICS: SOCIAL JUSTICE WARRIORS AND BEYOND

SOCIAL JUSTICE WARRIORS SPEND an inordinate amount of time attacking with vitriol those things (people, systems, and institutions) that they believe are responsible for bringing about the current difficult reality of the poor. As stated before, observing a problem is not the same as bringing workable solutions. Unbridled and unlimited anger is not a unifier in and of itself. Left unchecked, it denigrates and harms others, leading to division, hostility, and anarchy.

For some who call themselves anarchists, they believe that every structure that exists must be destroyed in order to bring about a better society with real justice. The anarchists naively say this as they communicate with each other on their corporate-built cellphones, communicating via social media platforms run by giant tech conglomerates, while using bear spray in their protests that was manufactured in China and shipped over on a boat owned by another corporation—all to move forward their agenda.

SOLUTIONS MINDSET: FOCUS ON THE SOLUTIONS, NOT INJUSTICE

The most effective way to engage people of a need for change is fivefold:

1. Clearly identify and articulate a problem.

2. Identify specific, workable solutions.

3. Implement the solutions in a planned, participatory way demonstrating the efficacy of the outcome.

4. Codify, refine, and communicate the success.

5. Enable continued success through legislation if necessary.

LIMITED MODEL OF SOLUTIONS: GOVERNMENT ONLY

Something must be done! Most social justice warriors advocate for more government intervention without realizing that most of the problems they are observing are caused by governments, whether local or international. The government becomes the primary path of solution for many because it has power and large resources that could be used to implement change by mandate something very attractive to the current crowd of social justice warriors. However, by employing the failing government systems that have caused and perpetuated the problems in the first place, the social justice warriors want to utilize and expand the reach of these same failed structures that we all want to improve. It is like giving a thief the keys to your house and asking them to watch it for you.

More importantly, the so-called "new solutions" demanded are based on *reacting* to old outcomes, while promoting the same old solutions that brought about the current undesired results. The existing problems will only be exacerbated if we do not critically examine the existing structures, laws, and systems bolstering the complex policies and systems that are the creators of the injustice in the first place. Just as adding money to the existing structures will only multiply the corruption, placing more money in the hands of those who steal money does not increase the amount going to the poor.

SOLUTIONS

Personal autonomy and freedom in a functional marketplace with access to capital are the best forms of liberating people from poverty while advancing accountability and sustainability. This way, the individual has authority over their own fate, as opposed to someone else faraway in a bureaucratic hierarchy commanding what is best for them and doling it out aid in small and inconsistent streams. In that old way of doing things, individuals are subordinated to corrupt government structures, policies, and practices; even those "designed" to alleviate injustice or abolish it will inevitably have features that will unintentionally or intentionally bring about new injustices, which benefit those paying the highest bribes. This is not cynicism—it is reality.

Since this thought goes against much of popular social justice thinking and rhetoric in this time of history, let us unpack it.

Facile Government-Solution Path

When social justice warriors see a big problem, their first natural impulse is to get a big government entity with adequate authority and large resources to address the problem. This is not just an issue for the social justice crowd, as it is a commonly shared sentiment among people as they examine their respective societal challenges and conclude, "The government should do something." This statement often ends the discussion and passes the responsibility onto someone else, too often eliminating our positive and essential participation in the change process.

Instead of creating even more inflexible government rules, we must liberate the creative ability of individuals to change their circumstance through hard work, which they both control and directly benefit from in the marketplace (i.e., capitalism). Empowering people to humbly serve the interests of others through commerce—thereby acquiring customers, making a wage, and creating long-term wealth—is the pathway to human flourishing through the marketplace.

When an area of ministry, government, or business is attacked by a bad actor, unjust system, or powerful exploiter, we reflexively develop new policies, systems, and procedures to avoid the same problem developing again. However, the law of unintended consequences also informs us that today's solution is the foundation of tomorrow's problem. Even our best intended solutions can quickly be manipulated by bad actors to become the foundation for future malfeasance, facilitated by incompetence, tethered to good intentions.

Even if our current legislative action cannot completely void the problem from occurring again in the future, we press on undeterred with our ever-growing and complex systems, ripe for manipulation and abuse. We naively create policies and procedures that are optimistically designed to deliver justice in an efficient and fair way, with the goal that the harm of a current bad situation is alleviated—only to discover that the hearts of humans are desperately wicked, and without Christ they creatively devolve the new structure into a new and creative corruption. A passionate Christ follower does not need laws to create morality; they will behave better than the law dictates because they live under the law of grace, fed by love and compassion, which nurture restorative and participatory justice as a natural outflowing.

BEWARE POSITIVE POLICIES' (UNINTENDED) NEGATIVE OUTCOMES

Most bad policy and legislation are exclusively and intently focused against the perceived perpetrators of a problem. Meanwhile, they ignore the secondary and tertiary effects on other innocent parties or the rest of the group, who will be adversely affected, often without any proof or substantiation that the new rules will actually halt the existing problem. It is not possible to make a law against every bad outcome and practice of bad virtue; they simply grow and multiply out of the woodwork. Most often the bad offender has already broken a law, but the knee-jerk reaction is to pass more laws in hopes of preventing further violations. Why would a corrupt person care about a new law while already breaking an existing one? Again, laws do not create or transform character.

Virtue

Character qualities like integrity, fairness, honesty, compassion, and justice are the foundations of a great society and functional markets. Character is not a result of legislation. Passing a law against something does not mean it will cease; in fact it may grow now that more people become curious about this thing that we passed a law against. Legislation at its best can bring consequences. However, it will not change a single human soul—of the oppressed, the oppressor, or anyone in between.

Totalitarians gain power through manipulating the struggles of the victims of a society to gain personal power and then manipulate others for their own enrichment. Once again, this comes at the expense of the vulnerable, who find themselves in an even worse state than before they were "helped."

OBSERVATION ON POLICY

Most policies that I have reviewed for many different businesses and organizations have features that unwittingly obstruct or eliminate the contributions of many of an organization's best workers, volunteers, or even the generous business owners who want to bless their employees. As counterintuitive as that sounds, it is the reality.

Bad policy, like bad legislation, is not regularly written to be bad. Bad policy is often written by hurt people who are so devastated by what just happened that they want to erect a permanent, impenetrable wall of protection by means of this policy. Thus, the bad behavior will be rendered helpless and the offending party's bad behavior will be impossible to repeat in the future.

PRACTICES:

1. As a rule, always apply your new legislation or policy to your most trusted team members, friends, and acquaintances to determine how it would affect them. This is a good stopgap in preventing unhelpful policy from proceeding, as it will be discovered that the new policy penalizes those who had nothing to do with the prior problem or behavior. Apply it to the best, and it will serve the rest.

2. Review existing policy and procedure to see if there are any gaps, errors, or omissions that helped lead to the current confusion. If so, fix them first before adding a new layer.

3. Understand that bad actors, abusers, and people of poor character will seek out and find new ways around the new and existing standards. This occurs because they lack integrity, not because the rules are unclear or imprecise.

WRITING PERFECT RULES AND REGULATIONS

The reality is that rules, policies, and laws do not in themselves stop bad behaviors or change character. This simply cannot be done through rule making, no matter the penalty. Likewise, the new policy will likely create an unintended new loophole for injustice or a rash indiscretion, either directly or indirectly. Character is only changed by conversion. When a person meets Jesus Christ, and the Spirit of God is given authority, amazing and miraculous change can happen. There are also spiritual encounters throughout our lives where things are reordered, or a painful loss ensues that causes us to rethink and reorient. Again, these are not because a new rule was passed. Also, unenforced rules or rules without consequences may as well not exist, and giving people repeated chances to improve only opens the door to future violation and harm. The best procedure for violators is to retrain, reassign, and remove.

Hint

When writing policy in the midst of a conflict situation, consider the application of the policy to your best employee, leader, or volunteers. I had a director bring me a proposed policy after a protracted conflict that had ended badly. Although the team leading the ministry department had correctly sought reconciliation, met with the person, and worked toward resolution, they had been stonewalled at every point. And even though the policy was clearly stated and direct (something all policies should be), it also had unintended consequences, just as all policies do (whether perceived or not). This particular policy built high walls of exclusion and was missing any form of reconciliation, which we will cover in another section.

The Test

In order to help this director to lessen the severity of the policy written to extricate any possibility of a recurrence, I began naming people on the team who had great hearts and selfless spirits that anyone would want to keep on their team. The impact to the people whose names were mentioned was clear, and the response of the director was appropriate: "It was not written for them. It was written for this other person."

"I understand that," I said, "but this is 'the policy,' so it applies across the whole department, to all people in the department, past, present, and future." I could see the light going on and the realization on his face, so I continued. "This policy could well keep many good people away from your department in the future, and you could lose some of your best people, those you value, because this applies to everyone."

Government policies can be the same, and when there is a government function, there is a large scale of application and consequences. Thus, the repercussions can range across multiple industries, people groups, and sectors and have significant financial implications. What does this mean? Where there are significant financial effects, people will find ways around the policy, edict, law, or regulation through seemingly benign organizations and structures that form to meet the new demands of the law. Rich people can hire lawyers, relocate purchases or businesses, and make bribes. Wealthy people have options created by their resources that are not available to others of lesser means, so now they have an increased advantage created by the combination of wealth and the new law. These malformations may be deleterious to the local economy overall; some will be corrupt or more corrupt than those that preceded the new law or policy.

POWER INEQUITIES

There is a regular *false belief* that a current injustice is ensconced solely in Colonialism displayed in the "power inequity" of the existing organizations, businesses, social classes, races, or personalities who run them, and that all those involved in the former or existing "dominant group" in these situations where these past power inequities are the root of all corruption or injustice. In fact, if you are not part of the majority power group, you are by definition deemed incapable of prejudice or corruption. However, systemic injustice regularly exhibits and points to an overall system of participatory corruption and dysfunction that people at all levels are actively participating in—whether willingly and overtly or blindly and naively. Either way the injustice prevails. The hoped-for solution is a political messiah from above, a new president or prime minister, who will end corruption at all levels and bring about a just and fair society where all bribes and payoffs are eliminated—"except the ones I count on. . ."

If a cashew-processing business were to open in a developing country like Nigeria, once it was successful, the government officials would come looking for hefty bribes and payoffs of 30 percent or more. So, the business shuts down, the employees are left without jobs, and the business owner is blamed as being greedy, unethical, or incompetent.

ADDRESSING CORRUPTION WITH CORRUPTION (SUBSTITUTING EVIL FOR EVIL)

So, let us say that a particular country has its major shipping port controlled by a single entity. It may be a corporation that has gained a monopoly interest through various political relationships, and potentially exploitative practices, to benefit those who pay the bribe and drive out the business of any small competitors who do not pay homage and cash to the established power base.

The simple thought is to remove the entity that currently controls the port, and justice will automatically ensue and prevail. But this system is built on corruption; everyone within the system has participated in the corruption at some level or another. Whatever the case may be, such participation has taken place, and replacing one ruling entity with another will not suffice as a solution. If there is a pile of fertilizer with a blue hat sitting on top of it, you can exchange the blue hat for a red one, but the pile of fertilizer is still a pile of fertilizer.

Many social justice advocates argue that assigning someone from a lower status—who benefitted the least from the prior corrupt organization or oligarchy—will automatically bring about justice, as they are part of the less fortunate, oppressed "pure class." Instead, it just places a new head on top of a corrupt system. It won't be long before this person sees the benefits in it being "their turn" to reap the bounty for themselves from the system.

Being oppressed or poor does not equate to intrinsic character or nobility; rather it merely accedes to the level of power of the individual at that time and condition. Someone at the lowest level takes the lowest bribe, not because of their superior character but because of their station in the hierarchy of bribes. If promoted, they will more than likely take the next highest bribe in the system, and so on. Systemic evil and poor character are forever entwined with each other.

IS CHANGE HOPELESS?

Change is hopeful and real, but it requires special diligence by those with character and fortitude to achieve it. What about extra policing of the port to prevent corruption? All that does is add a new layer of bribery payments to the corrupt system that is still in place. If one takes the bribe, all take the bribe.

Space does not permit a writing of new policy, but a structure of questions to ask to achieve it does. Here are a few questions to ask to set up the structure for a new system to inhibit corruption (a hope and a dream). Also note that eliminating corruption will regularly require replacing everyone in the system—a daunting task that has its own implications and pitfalls.

Prompts for the Port Challenge

1. What are the structures and passageways that currently exist for cargo? Who controls them?

2. Create procedures that allow for incoming and outgoing cargo that are transparent and can easily be used by all.

3. Develop blind procedures for processing cargo, both incoming and outgoing, that favor only potential spoilage of product and not preferential treatment (e.g., firms doing business under the auspices of the government or those paying bribes).

4. Create neutral practices, one for cargo entering and another for cargo leaving.

5. Replace all staff if the policy changes are not effective.

ESTABLISH OPEN AND ACHIEVABLE STANDARDS

Until the Christians in a society prayerfully repent of their own participation in the systems of bribery, corruption, and payoffs, nothing will change. The false self-absolution given for receiving relatively small payoffs and bribes is not a solution towards effective reform; rather it only exacerbates the problem. Likewise, singling out blame for those at the top who take the biggest bribes will not change the system either. In fact, this is another way of self-absolving utilized by those lower down in the system of corruption for taking their piece, which in the end robs everyone. All of this is further rationalized by the statement of how poor the individual is and how they deserve at least "a little something-something." Until we weep over our collusion in the corruption, change will not begin.

Determine Pathways: Port Example

1. What and who are the parties than can ship products from our country?

2. Whom do they need to go though (what entities, persons, and structures) to export or import?

3. What is the maximum time that cargo can be detained, and for what specific reasons? How are these conditions ascertained? What is the right of protest, appeal, or grievance that exists? What is the penalty for the one who signs off on the cargo being detained unfairly?

4. How can this system be flattened to increase access and widened participation in order to allow access to foreign markets—even to the smallest entity without bribes—so our ports may serve as neutral entry points?

5. What imports are key to our expansion and utilization of indigenous natural resources?

6. Are there third parties seeking to harm our industries with exploitative or unfair trade practices?

7. What would be the time limit for reviewing or sunsetting any actions taken to rectify this situation once reform is achieved?

8. Who are the international partners (power brokers, former/new colonial powers, business interests) who have sway over the control of our shipping? Are their interests in alignment to ours, or are they placing undue burdens on our country that need to be addressed?

43

Policy with Restoration

DIAGNOSIS

CORRUPTION IS THE STICKY tar of inefficiency that clings to our feet with every step we take, leaving an indelible stain on the carpet of our culture, economy, and body politic. This results in waste, destruction, and corruption for the purpose of benefiting a small group that steals off of the majority a disproportionate piece of the revenue from a crippled, stifled system, of which they are both the masters and the victims.

CAUSE

Businesspeople cooperate with corrupt governments and government officials, and they work together. Governments extort bribes and payoffs, which reduce income and increase risk, so businesses seek protections from competition to shore up their market share and bring inflated prices to the market to cover the assigned risk of the bribes, payoffs, and extortion. This is accomplished through legislation or favorable treatment for themselves, and unfavorable treatment for potential competitors—further justifying the ongoing bribes and corruption in the view of the government officials' stance ("Look what we have done for you"). The government officials are motivated to take as much as they can from current systems, believing that the resources available are limited to what currently exists, and that the only way for them to prosper is to remove, reassign, or steal as many things as possible so they will prosper. Those who participate in this system at any level simply believe that potentially their "turn" will come one day, and when it does, they will have their opportunity at the trough of personal excess along with those who belong to their tribe.

CURE: OVERCOME POVERTY THINKING

"This is all there is. I better get mine." This limited-opportunity worldview is a set of assumptions based on a poverty mindset. Even those people getting rich off this system are acting like beggars at the table, trying to fill their plate by grabbing little scraps from the plates of others so that their plate will be full.

The reality is, given the freedom to exercise their ability, there are more plates to be made and more opportunities to be filled—more food to be grown, more cooking to be accomplished, more feasting to be enjoyed—when we set out with an abundance mindset geared toward expansion, multiplication, and wealth building for the society. All social systems without the necessary, commonly shared high morals that are put into practice every day denigrate into the thievery of individuals and groups in hopes of personally thriving at the expense of others.

Many social justice advocates truncate their thinking around governmental, legislative solutions, believing that unless the larger society creates rules and mandates of benevolence and equity, justice will not reign. But these well-intended efforts fail because a small group of elites become the arbiters of what is best for the society, and inevitably, they and their offspring receive the best of all things, as they "care" for the entrapped lower peoples from their permanent, lofty places of power and influence. Command and control economies result from these actions, and they fail due to their inability to react creatively in the multiplicity of ways that individuals do on a daily basis to adapt to changing circumstances. A society and its economic outputs are too complex to be managed by a single, central bureau or government agency. Human beings are finite; bureaucratic managers sift about with partial knowledge of existing systems and structures, but free markets have individuals who innovate solutions before bureaucrats can accurately identify the problems. Addressing complex systems with governmental powers quickly delves into the depths of human depravity and greed through political self-interests and artificial structures that are based on power and payoffs—not efficiency, productivity, and the growing societal wealth and profits of an expanding marketplace of opportunity.

Socialism is regularly and reflexively embraced as the quickest and most thorough replacement solution for a former corrupt country ruled by king, queen, tsar, or president for life. However, it is merely replacing the leadership of an already socialist, authoritarian structure with more of the same. Having a system that states equality as its basis is attractive to those who have only experienced inequality. In the end the new ruling class—which replaces the blood line of the former dynastic rulers with a new blood line of designated, non-dynastic rulers under the auspices of "caring for the people"—consistently has the same poor outcomes. It is grotesque hubris when people believe they will be the new, truly ethical people wielding unlimited power.

It is Machiavellian at its roots, as a presumed "superior" elite now replaces the former elites via a moral primacy and practice, which while stating to serve the people, leaves the poor and disenfranchised to remain where they were before—with very few notable exceptions. As the ruling class gain ascendancy and their command policies stifle the economy, the ruling class quips, "This is the price we all must pay for a system of equality and justice." However, this white robe of prurient rhetoric falls apart when you enter the homes of the elite in these "societies of equality" and discover that the opulent equality that they experience renders actual equality to be a mirage—effectively limiting the upward opportunities of those not currently included in the classes of the "benevolent elite."

Naively focusing on promoting authoritarian (because they have authority) socialistic structures, which theoretically promote the achieving of equal or "improved and superior" societal outcomes, fails by design. So-called equal outcomes are an imposter of actually improving living standards, which can be accomplished through empowering the poor by releasing people's talents and potential in an open, systemic, and sustainable way that protects property, creativity, access to markets, and autonomy.

PIZZA PARADIGM

If the goal of a society is to deliver the best-tasting, most economical pizza to everyone in the society, that may be a worthy goal, unless there is someone who does not like pizza. In this case, pizza becomes oppressive to this person, a resource they do not want, or desire is administered to them from afar instead of something they long for. Although simplistic, the principle is comprehendible.

Those who advocate for socialism in its many forms will protest, 'But we are not trying to deliver pizza but food security for all!" However, most are unwilling to admit when their systems and structures of so-called justice fail; instead they blame everyone and everything, except themselves and their failed system, to support achieving the exception to the rule of socialism's failures. Again the toxic and malignant hubris emerges: "This time it will work because our hearts are purer than all those who have gone before us."

"The heart is hopelessly dark and deceitful a puzzle that no one can figure out. But I, God, search the heart and examine the mind. I get to the heart of the human. I get to the root of things. I treat them as they really are, not as they pretend to be" (Jeremiah 17:19, The Message).

The same failed systems that benefit a small elite class economically and socially are the ultimate outcomes in an impoverish society with little opportunity, no upward mobility, and an economy of stagnation. These are all that is truly being offered or ever delivered.

When discussing socialism, those in the West regularly look at Europe and Asia and the communist socialist countries of the last hundred years (always excluding Nazi Germany). Rarely do they think of the current African economies that suffer under the thriving of the governments' invasive control in the socialist and quasi-socialist countries that exist there. Even though they may not always call themselves socialist, their systems of central control and what is commonly called "planning" all smack of high-level government control, which is so rampant and economically stifling. This pervasive involvement in every aspect of society, including the economy, is just another failed variant of socialism. The prime international goal of their leaders is to prop up their failed fiefdoms by appealing to the "wealthy nations" to have compassion on the "poor, developing nations," which demand increasing aid support from the West until they can grow sufficiently in the future. However, their systems of corruption prevent that very same future from arriving. Every door of opportunity is controlled by the government and only opened with a bribe—and even then, just a crack.

The true advocates of socialism who are often among the modern-day "social justice advocates" will cringe at these corrupt and unjust regimes being lumped in with their utopian ideas of socialism, where birds are chirping, springs are flowing, the air is clean, and everyone has a PhD and drives a Prius (or better yet, takes the train).

Why are we discussing socialism in a book on community development and local, systemic economic transformation?

COMMON THREAD OF AID: TRANSFER PAYMENTS

Much of the aid, development, and relief work done by governments, NGOs, charities, and churches is done from a socialist understanding that focuses on *transfer payments* from wealthy to poor. This model obviates the invigorating and liberating practices of creating a climate of economic opportunity through local people's individual and team creativity, ingenuity, and wealth creation. These are the practices that have raised so many communities from poverty in the modern era.

Conversely, every good and well-intended aid solution that goes through a government system will experience a huge portion of the resources disappearing in administrative and other costs, and their involvement will ultimately destroy the outcome. This is not cynicism; it is historic, documented outcomes.

CORRUPTION: NEED FOR CAPITAL

One of the major keys to economic expansion and success is peoples' access to capital. One of the major causes of poverty is a lack of access to capital. Land is a form of capital that can be used to produce crops or house the buildings for a business or private home. In many countries, land ownership with clear legal title is a matter that is always in question. In these countries one gets land to farm from the local chief or the paramount chief. This transaction may be conducted over a few beers, which the individual pays for, and is completed by a handshake. However, if ownership and clear title are the issue, the price changes, as do the terms. But the technical procedure stays the same, and one may never receive title or legal documentation to establish legitimate ownership. Or if they do, it is not defendable in court, and any government entity can seize it at any time, by fiat.

With clear title to land, a farmer can go to the bank and borrow money for a tractor, using the land as collateral. Without the title, the farmer has no collateral, and the bank will not make the loan. So, how can you get a tractor without title to the land that you have been farming for decades?

Tractor Project

Malawi was given a gift of 400 tractors by the Indian government. The purpose of the tractors was to increase productivity in rural areas that did not have access to this kind of machinery. The tractors arrived and were distributed around the country. However, they fell under the authority of local politicians, and each one became located on the land of national politicians in their home villages. After a few years, it was determined that these tractors were not being used as originally envisioned and specified. A special investigation ensued, and when the larger report of the investigation was presented on the use of the tractors, it was determined that the tractors were not able to be located.

I asked one of my partners why the tractors weren't being used for any business. *Why not rent them out?* He said because the tractors had gone missing and were "officially" being searched for, the politicians who had taken them for their own use had to keep them hidden and couldn't let them out for rental, because that would identify where the tractor was and would place them in a potentially criminal situation.

Systemic corruption is not a small thing. In fact, it has tentacles into everything. Corruption also limits everything. It destroys transportation by making inferior roads that fail. It clogs courts with cases that will be endlessly delayed (justice delayed is justice denied). It creates excessive fees and taxes that deny people products they could otherwise afford and use to make a living, and it limits their access to export markets. Government corruption in essence is stabbing these countries' economies in the heart.

44

Corruption Metastasizes
How It Invades

THE CHALLENGE WITH CORRUPTION is that when it is played out cultur-ally in significant ways, it has multiple participants in every facet of life—in both government and industry. Corruption functions as a debilitating drain of production on the larger economy, as a sub-economy or dark economy that undermines and destroys the dominant economy. This is perhaps the crucial part that participants do not fully comprehend, or if they do, they view their tiny part of the bribe to be inconsequential in the scope of the larger economy. "What could this small amount I re-ceive possibly hurt?" goes the thought. "Anyway, others take much larger bribes. Go after them. I am just trying to get by."

Each bribe and each payoff—no matter how small—is a cancer cell traveling through the economy, destroying its ability to grow and thrive. It cripples everything that it touches, and it negates future healthy growth.

FALSE HOPE NEVER DELIVERED

All the while this dark sub-economy offers up a false hope of financial increase while surreptitiously tearing down every new opportunity for economic expansion. It does this by fighting over the current resources and limiting expansion due to the heavy burden that this corrupt system places on new medium-size businesses. Amazingly, all of this destruction is accomplished against the poor *by* the many poor actively participating via the small tips received, creating the foundation of the system that supports the few who garner the biggest bribes by their profligate exploitation of their position. But in the end, it leaves a gaping hole in these tattered economies that would otherwise be occupied by production and fruitful expansion.

IT TAKES A VILLAGE

Supported by the lowliest secretary or clerk, to the head of a corporation, and all the government officials and their hirelings—everyone gets at least a little piece. Everyone gets a little taste. Everyone is part of building the wall and foundations that protect what is going wrong, while destroying and blockading increased productivity. All of this happens at the expense of functional commerce, due to the greed of government officials, who sincerely believe that they deserve to have a piece of everything that they come into contact with yet had no part in actually creating. Ironically, this behavior limits not only how big their piece of the pie could be but how many more pies could be created (or the relative size of the economy). Often and inevitably, they are actually shrinking the potential for the larger graft that is so alluring by the shortsightedness of their debilitating greed, when there could be so much more opportunity in size, scope, and function by taking less and allowing commerce to flourish without their toxic and unnecessary intervention.

THE BIG LIE

The great deception of corruption is that the small bribes that most people receive in these systems are perceived as being benign or having no deleterious effect. *After all, how could they have any real affect when they are so small?* This is the great lie. The tentacles of participating in this system reach into everything and destroy it—like a tumor growing and crowding out all the healthy organs and affecting every healthy tissue—crippling the whole life of the economy. Sipping on the poison of the bribe or payoff infects every individual who participates, and the poison metastasizes into the society, making sickness more normal than health, and death more certain than expansion and a healthy, long life.

Absolution for the Small Bribe

Incidentally, it is the biggest thieves in the systems, taking millions and billions from the economy for their personal benefit, who bring a sort of absolution to those taking the smaller bribes and payoffs. "At least I am not as bad as them. I would never take that kind of money." And so the thinking goes.

Corruption limits technology, destroys supply chains, limits production and competition, while allowing a few to "succeed" through bribery, graft, and corruption at the cost of the vast majority.

Corrupt systems go hand in hand with socialist/authoritarian governments, particularly in controlling and extorting trade. Access to markets and importation in these systems are generally controlled by a single entity, for the sake of "efficiency and accountability" against corruption. One of the best solutions to corruption is fair and open markets with transparent processes. Yet these kinds of socialist governments regularly give favorable cover to exploitative government monopolies and favored businesses, particularly when they partner together in joint ventures. But these practices exploit the people who work in them for poverty wages, and they strangle the creativity and ingenuity of the populace of those countries.

COCOA CARTELS

As stated before, cocoa farmers around the world get less than one-tenth of a penny from the retail sale of a dollar's worth of chocolate sold. Without their production of cocoa, there would be no chocolate, but they are forced to go through processors and shipping/transport businesses that control both the market and the price paid for the unprocessed cocoa.

Anyone who complains or seeks to dry or refine their cocoa product independently will find themselves at odds with the cartel and the port authority—left with a product that they are unable to sell. They will then effectively be banned from the cocoa cooperative and denied access to all cocoa markets. There will be no port access for their product and no one else to buy it, lest they also be economically "canceled." The offender will effectively be put out of business by the cartel that controls cocoa.

This is what socialist governments bring in the name of equality for all and a living wage. Instead, people receive oppression of their livelihood, and the profits available are skewed to those in power. Likewise, the creativity of individuals to improve society through innovation, new solutions, and value-adding expansion is suppressed, leaving everyone less well-off. The only exception is those on the top, who in these systems are permanently ensconced as the ruling class. This comes in stark contrast to dynamic, open markets where there is a near-constant movement upward, and people are seeking to join in from the bottom with plans for growth.

Yet, there are a few fighting this corrupt monopoly. One chocolate shop in San Luis Obispo, California, has been buying cocoa directly from farmers for over fifteen years, but this buyer is now aging out of the business and plans to retire. New entrepreneurs must arise to fill the gaping voids in this and other economic situations globally.

45

Fighting Corruption

WE HAVE SEEN HOW corruption works in control (i.e., socialist) economies. The next step in analyzing the problem is to determine who is actually participating and keeping the corruption going.

Who is participating? *Almost everyone*. It may be a slight exaggeration to say that "everyone" participates in corruption in economies that utilize government-controlled systems, have high levels of corruption, and allow secondary markets. But the participation is at all levels, and the payments are distributed widely. From the official who takes the bribe to the clerk at the counter, there is a little bit for everyone, and the passing of envelopes containing money is more common than a greeting or handshake.

In the public market, items are bought and sold, food is delivered to stores and shops, and customers purchase it. But in the background, there is a black or gray market where bribes are paid, mafia groups are given a kickback, and bandits on the road extort a fee for "safe travel."

NAIL BOARDS AND "FEE COLLECTION"

In traveling from an African capital city to one of the nearby cities, everyone in our party was instructed to deposit our money in a bank for our two-hour trip across the countryside. The idea was that after we had reached our destination, we could remove the money from the bank and wouldn't have to worry about it being stolen by bandits along the way.

While we were on our drive in our van, we came around a blind turn, and two men threw a nail-studded board out in front of our vehicle, so we came to an abrupt stop. These men asked to see the registration for the vehicle but were unwilling to produce any kind of identification as to their authority. Upon inspection these men determined that the registration for the vehicle would be up soon, so it was imperative that the registration be paid to them, at that place and at that time. A long discussion ensued with significant volume in vocalization and waving of hands and the holding of weapons on the waist to intimidate.

In the end we paid them the money that they were asking for, or some amount negotiated close to it, after we had been on the side of the road for at least an hour trying to wait each other out. The documents were stamped by something that they were holding in their hand in a haphazard way, and we continued on our journey. This is not unusual.

Ultimately, we were fortunate that those who had stopped us did not try to rob us individually as well. In fact they initially thought we were businesspeople because we were too well dressed to be missionaries as our hosts claimed us to be. Although once identified as missionaries, we were treated with greater deference, a testament to the sacrificial work that missionaries have contributed in the past and the honor that they have achieved.

In today's climate in many countries, it would be entirely possible for someone to be kidnapped for ransom. All of this is part of and consequent to the system of corruption. There are some who say that with prosperity these particular acts would no longer be necessary. Although I would like to agree, these comments are naive and do not take into account the stranglehold that this corruption produces on the minds of people trapped in these corrupt and hopeless systems. Not only is the economy wildly distorted, but there is also a significant distortion created in people's thinking about their lives and future. It comes not only from these circumstances but from inside of people themselves.

People I have met were asked by their kidnappers to pray for them as they were releasing them, claiming they only did these things because they had no other choice. Deep down, they sense something is wrong, and they long for personal redemption. Although we are describing the failed corruption of socialistic systems and emphasizing advocacy for economic freedom and change in this section, its success is ultimately and relentlessly tied to the redemption of souls. Otherwise, from the ransom that the kidnappers receive, they will pay bribes to the police, and all of them will continue to play their assigned parts in an unhealthy system of poverty, control, and corruption. Only through the hope of Christ and the freedom to live and bless others through their gifts will there be invigorating, sustainable change.

FIGHTING CORRUPTION

One of these African countries, in an effort to thwart its own endemic corruption, decided to set up an Office of Anti-Corruption and asked a well-respected community leader to consider taking the job. However, he was informed that the bribe necessary to get the job as chief of the anti-corruption office was $16,000. To Westerners, that will be shocking; to those who live in these systems, they will smile and say, "Of course."

Only the Church Can Change It

The church is the only entity that can change society and see an end to this corruption. Believers must be the ones who say no to the bribes, both individually and corporately. This will be costly, and they must be willing to accept the pain and persecution that will follow as they take a stand against this cancerous evil. The sacrifice is worth it to free their people and economies from the tyranny of the boiling cauldron of theft, graft, and corruption that are destroying their lives and those of their children.

46

The Aid Industry and the
Effects of Corruption

CORRUPTION HAS A VARIETY of primary and secondary effects that it creates in the aid industry, which seeks to fight this very corruption through
various mechanisms as the monies move through the system in a variety
of ways. The following are just some of those ways.

#1: DILUTION OF FUNDS

The dominant organizations that receive grants (e.g., UNICEF, World
Vision, Compassion International, Catholic charities) have those grants
funded from a government entity to their entity or NGO. Then those
monies often go through another national or local government branch
within the local country before they reach the project site where the
people in need are. By the time those monies have arrived at the local site,
they have been depleted by well over half in a system of bloated structures, as well as growing graft and corruption that run in many different
directions, having their own written and unwritten rules for payments up
the chain of command. Likewise, the NGOs have often burdensome accountability protocols prescribed by the donor or granting organizations
up the food chain, which waste 10 to 20 percent and more in completing

redundant compliance reports weekly, monthly, and quarterly. These forms are then the subject and spectacle of relentless foreign audits.

#2: EXCLUDING INDIGENOUS GOVERNMENT PARTICIPATION

To avoid the graft in the local government passthroughs and the wasteful bureaucracies created to "assist" aid organizations in their work, some organizations now refuse to partner with receiving governments in any way, creating a further separation between Western intelligentsia's control and the inclusion of the local people in their own solutions. By obviating the voice of their governments and local leaders, and by replacing them with "Western experts," there is no constructive coordination of efforts, nor utilization of invaluable local knowledge. In this way the goal of local autonomy over the destiny of a village, family, or individual is once again far removed from the people themselves; it is instead vested in the expert decision makers at the United Nations in New York or legislators in London, Belgium, or Washington, DC to take charge with their degrees, prestige, and bureaucratic knowledge.

However, the best experts on any problem are the people from the place where the problem exists. They are the greatest stakeholders. They have the greatest knowledge about their communities. They are the ones who are invested in the outcomes being successful because the problem affects their families and community directly. This change can only be achieved and sustained when the right local leaders are in place.

#2B: ALTERNATE MODEL

An alternate model is to strategically *empower local leaders* directly, to give them the exposure to options as well as the necessary tools and co-operatively designed business models that they need to see these positive things happen. Here again, the key is identifying a reliable and ethical local leader who has the interests of the community first.

#2C CHALLENGE: FALSE LEADERS

There are many false people out there who have a great "line" to share, sad stories to tell you, and can even take you to a location where they claim to be working. Many times this is all a mirage. A few years ago I was eating breakfast in a hotel restaurant in Cairo and saw a person who fit this description—flitting about the buffet table with a keen smile and a predator's eyes alongside a well-intentioned, white American taking it all in, listening attentively, and being drawn into the scam.

The correction for these duplicitous deceptions is for the local leader model to be employed as described here to work effectively. It is to *partner with local leaders that you have known* for a period of time in your own context, where you have observed their life and fruit. Of course, this is easier said than done. I have had the good fortune of traveling to over 40 countries in my life, and I know leaders from all over the world and sit on the board of a seminary that is devoted to educating international students from around the globe. I get to meet the best of the best, and the rest.

There is no shortcut in identifying a high-quality, local leader and building a healthy, mutual relationship with them and the community that they are from. This process can take from one to three years. But the benefits last for many years and will multiply into other communities and leaders, if cultivated effectively. The fruit is tremendous, but as with a fruit tree, it takes years before you see the harvest come to fruition. However, once it gets going, it has its own momentum and brings forth more fruit than could be imagined. It far outshines the current practices of dolling out small sums relentlessly over a prolonged period, merely sustaining the local poverty situation at a slightly higher level.

47

The Local Church's Key
Role in the Fight

NEW LAWS FAIL CORRUPT HEARTS

LAWS DO NOT CHANGE a corrupt heart. New laws are merely another
obstacle for the corrupt heart to work around in order to achieve their
self-serving ends. Even great systems operated by corrupt people are
eventually destroyed. John Adams said of the U.S. Constitution that the
system would only work if it was administered by a moral people.[1] We
can see the results today of that lack and the obsession with adding more
laws in the hopes that those breaking the existing laws will somehow be
reformed or deterred by the addition of new legislation. Laws can abate
some symptoms, but they cannot change a human heart.

The Western and governmental approaches to abating corruption
in the aid industry focus on specific strategies, procedural reporting,
processes, laws, and rules that only further complicate the problem to
be addressed. This obtuse string of time-wasting practices creates a web
of irrelevant, redundant, and fruitless systemic structures that stifle creative enterprise and economic expansion. Likewise, their ineffectiveness
results in the relentless additions of even more of the same in the hopes
of garnering a different outcome. This glorious new regulation, we are

1. Adams, "Letter from John Adams," para. 3.

promised, will be the one that ultimately stops the relentless theft of resources that we all dread. . . until it does not.

FIGHTING LOCAL CORRUPTION

What if the local churches said to their people, "Don't give to the offering from your bribes"? Consider the effect if they would instead curse the money that comes from bribes, declaring that it chokes those who demand it as well as those who receive it. They would pray and repent while challenging and refusing these bribes. "Lord Jesus, please make the refusing of bribes a blessing in my office. Bless each one that says no to a bribe. . ." What effect might that prayer have on a society plagued by corruption?

WHERE FAILURE FOCUSES: PLACE BLAME AND PASS LAWS

Failure focuses on placing blame on specific institutions, governments, and individuals of power, wealth, and importance. It is forever pointing the finger outward but rarely looks inward. For most bribe takers, they see the small amount that they receive as innocuous in the process and instead focus on those who receive the largest amounts as the "truly evil" ones. They love to see these who have taken so much be publicly exposed in the media and savor the judgements of courts that come their way. Then the self-absolution again takes place: "Well, I have never taken that kind of money." In reality, they have taken the exact same kind of money, just in lesser amounts. It is like the man with one mistress criticizing the moral character of the man with five mistresses.

ANTI-CORRUPTION LAWS—SEEDBED OF NEW CORRUPTION

1. The Fraud: When large-scale fraud by a government official embezzling thousands or millions of dollars is exposed, the outrage and indignation is everywhere in the media.

2. The Response: Reflexively, people demand reform, and officials once again attempt to create laws to punish what everyone already knows is wrong. The new laws added atop the old ones are sure to

be the solution to preventing future fraud and wrongdoing by those in power.

3. The Embrace: Since the public is jealous that they will never receive such huge sums legally, they willingly go along with creating the new, complicated laws and structures, which make their own lives more difficult, even when these laws cost them jobs.

Then, It Happens Again. . .

When the next inevitable story of corruption hits the headlines, the cycle repeats. Never hoping to receive a million dollars in bribes or stolen funds, we become aware of someone who has, and we now protest again that "the government should do something." *We demand new laws!*

After all of this, does the corruption end? Sadly, the answer is no. Corrupt people find a new way to be corrupt.

National Plea

The complaints continue: "This multinational business is corrupt and partnered with the government." "They are taking advantage of us." "The system is not fair."

So, it is determined that current undesirable outcomes again necessitate even more useless laws, codes, and statutes to add to those already being violated. This creating even more cumbersome, convoluted, expensive, and stifling systems that everyone must wade through but that only those with expensive lawyers can overcome. For those who operate in an honest and ethical fashion, too bad—you, too, will be punished for the sins of others and must spend to comply with the new anticorruption laws, be subject to prosecution, or close your business. Perhaps you could pay a bribe instead and be granted amnesty. . .

The outcome is a worse system with contradictions and embedded loopholes that further the ambitions of the corrupt and their lawyers. Meanwhile, the undeliverable promise of justice, fairness, and good outcomes languishes in the pile of bureaucratic intricacies that bury the never-achieved dreams of millions of people.

International Plea

In response to this legislative and economic degradation caused by corruption, the government leaders of these nations go to the U.N. and make a speech about the need for more foreign aid. Their pleas echo the moral obligation of the world to aid them in their continued corruption because the problems tied to more cumbersome laws (meant to assuage the West) are causing the poor to cry out once again, and they must be helped with more of the same.

48

Doubling Down
International Request for Assistance

"GIVE US MORE MONEY, PLEASE"

THE INCREASING REQUESTS FOR donations and aid due to the suffering of the people under these economically restrictive and complicated systems, to be paid to and through the local governments, add to the graft and corruption that exacerbated and brought about the problem to begin with.

The plea to donors is "We must do something!" The charity says, "Give now or people will die."

OPTIONS AND ALTERNATIVES

- Option 1: Give even more to the ever-failing system of increasing aid and economic degradation.

- Option 2: Avoid the corruption by addressing a single "key" factor (e.g., wells for clean water, girls' education, etc.)

- Option 3 (Hope and Legislation): Hope that option 2 will miraculously fix the entire system, even though it has neither the ability nor the plan to do so. For example, still missing in the equation are young, educated graduates who have no jobs because the economy is stifled by oligarchical businesses and monopolies that control the opportunities available. Simultaneously, the quagmire of the

legislative world continues creating endless regulations, administered by complicated multi-office visits to start even the simplest
of businesses entities or to address basic permits, certifications, and
the like.

- Option 4: Churches, individuals, and organizations partner to directly invest in a community via a self-sustaining business model
that is mutually developed, locally administered, funded by local
businesses and economic expansion, and led by a local, independent board and a transformed and internationally exposed leader.

HOW POVERTY PROGRAMS DO THE SAME THINGS, EVEN IN GOD'S NAME

When food, clothing, and school services are supplied by outside sources,
they create increased future dependance. Without creating healthy infrastructure and capital for business creation and expansion, the poor
remain victims of circumstances, tied to the whims of donors and the
global climate, which can shift at any moment. The direct aid—whether
coming from a government or a charity—is a trap and a prison if it does
not provide economic opportunity for expansion.

"THE GOVERNMENT SHOULD DO SOMETHING. . ."

Everybody says it. Most people believe it. But does it work?

Here are questions that must be considered: What is the structure
of the solutions that the government is supposed to have? What sorts of
outcomes can reliably be expected? What are the other potentialities of
governmental involvement to be anticipated?

With consistent pleas of government involvement, there is a concomitant lack of personal responsibility, locally and globally, which results
in a certain level of abdication for participation as well as investment in potential outcomes. What if there is no governmental response even though
there is an outcry? There will only be inactivity and continued suffering.

CHRISTIAN RESPONSIBILITY

U.S. President John F. Kennedy' famously stated, "Ask not what your country can do for you—ask what you can do for your country."[1] Several action points emerge that we would do well to take to heart:

1. We all must take the responsibility to make our homes, churches, communities, cities, countries, and globe a better place, particularly where there is endemic injustice oppressing our brothers and sisters.

2. We must ask what our role in making them better at each level can be. How can my family make a difference? How can my church make a difference? How can my community make a difference. How can my country make a difference?

3. In asking these questions, we move toward actualizing resolve and building momentum toward making a difference because we are examining not only the goal but the talents, abilities, and influence of each group at each level.

4. Do not ask someone to do what they cannot do. Seeking governmental solutions for creative challenges places these managerial institutions in a quandary, as they are by design administrative and not creative.

MANAGERS AND ADMINISTRATORS

Governments naturally deal with legislation and its implementation. They maintain and run police forces, sewage plants, roads, and bridges. They are managers and administrators. The government is designed to care for shared services and systems that support the majority of the people. Do not ask the government to do something that it is not good at and was not designed for.

Creativity

Governments are not creative; they are managerial. Nor are they adept at creating competitive enterprises that build cars, trains, homes, or almost anything else that can be imagined. When governments build a

1. Kennedy, "President John F. Kennedy's," para. 5.

building, they hire a private architect, construction firm, landscape architects, paving companies, electricians, plumbers, and others—all under the authority of a general contractor to manage and organize the work efficiently. Likewise, to build a bridge, they hire engineering companies and construction companies. In order to get the best proposal, they allow companies to bid on projects competitively. This happens for everything, from the presidential limousine and office furniture to munitions and weapons. As these private companies compete, they are challenged to improve the product and keep costs down.

But realize that when the government is involved, the cost will be higher and the work less efficient. For example, a supervisor on the new construction of the Wilshire rapid-transit train tunnel told me that the costs for running the project the way the government wants cost 400 percent more and take three times as long.

RESOURCES ALONE ARE NOT THE CURE

Because governments deal with large sums of money, it is assumed that the government has the solutions or at least the potentiality of solutions to all of our problems. Competency to make positive change is not a corollary of the amount of money or power that one has. More money or resources do not equal more knowledge or better decision making in all areas. Having more resources does not mean having more ability or competence.

Large resources are still limited resources. Large resources do not mean an entity more readily notices the real problems of people. Often there is an inverse relationship between having authority over significant resources and noticing problems, as those in charge of the resource realize how little there is to go around in the end toward all the needs. It can become overwhelming to see so many problems and be limited in what one can do to help, given the constraints of the government's role, rules, regulations, and financial restrictions (not to mention corruption). Noticing problems does not mean that the necessary creative solutions are apparent to the one noticing—let alone that an effective solution will be produced even if the problems are noticed or addressed.

These challenges are described in the Bible: "If you see the poor oppressed in a district, and justice and rights denied, do not be surprised at such things; for one official is eyed by a higher one, and over them both are others higher still. The increase from the land is taken by all;

the king himself profits from the fields. Whoever loves money never has enough; whoever loves wealth is never satisfied with their income. This too is meaningless" (Ecclesiastes 5:8–10, NIV).

DEFINING GOVERNMENT AND FUNDING

What is government? It is a collective corporation formed by the body politic under a leadership or authority structure that has persuasive and retributive powers exercised through systems of law (not competition) over the society.

Q&A

Question: Does direct government funding, or government funding through an NGO providing aid, work efficiently to bring the desired results?

Answer: Funding through multiple third-party entities and governmental agencies tends to draw off large percentages of the intended resources for administrative and "other" purposes—often 70 percent or more.

Question: Do we need more funding to be more effective, as we regularly hear from government leaders?

Answer: Just because something is funded does not mean it is producing the desired results. Likewise, more funding will not necessarily increase the effectiveness or the number of people being assisted. This is assumed, since according to logic, more should equal more, but more may only apply to the corruption and graft that are at play.

Some Questions to Determine Project Effectiveness

1. What is the total expenditure for the program?
2. What percentage is being used before reaching the people that it is intended to assist?
3. What is the cost per person for each of the first three years?
4. When will the project be self-sufficient?
5. When will the project be profitable?
6. When will the project give birth to a new project?

7. Are we fostering corruption through efforts of justice?

8. Are the administrative costs of the government partnership preventing corruption, or are they adding to vice, corruption, and greed (whether or not the individuals themselves who administer these funds are ethical)?

49

Common Justice Beliefs and Biases

THREE ORGANIZATIONAL APPROACHES TO RECONSIDER

#1: Business Is Corruptly Partnered with Government (Break It Apart)

BUSINESS IS BAD, AND charity is good. This belief is all too common amongst individuals legitimately seeking justice in society. "The system is not fair," they say. "We must remove the corrupt link between business and government. Therefore, current and future outcomes mandate eliminating business and increasing socialism, since it is designed within the framework of positive fairness."

The fact that these solutions are even worse systems that are unable to deliver on their promises of good or improved outcome—that have never been achieved—is ignored, or we are told that the true form has never been tried. Finally, the great arrogance is added: "We will be different sorts of leaders of these systems when we implement them." This notion is truly naive and arrogant at the same time, as these systems have regularly had the same results. Far from bringing life, there are instead millions dead![1]

---

1. Courtois, *The Black Book of Communism*, 4.

#2: Departmental Focus (Government)

Here the solution is scaled down to focusing on the creation of a new departmental area to address poverty. The hope is that over time resources can be reallocated, and the local government can internally fund their own special poverty departments or create new departments to distribute resources and perform tasks. They can also audit to track particular costs and determine within a range how many or what kind of help, product, or service has been provided. They are stationary and nondynamic in function and culture. They are highly resistant to change, as they are not organized for innovation. Rather, their focus is on their own protocols, processes, and staffing structures. The unspoken goal is maintenance of the office and its function, whether or not it produces a benefit to the society.

#3: Individual/Recipient Focus (Aid Organizations)

Aid organizations primarily focus on the distribution of crisis aid, including but not limited to emergency food distribution, housing, clothing, medicine, and water. As aid organizations continue to work past the initial emergency state, they continue the individual focus of relieving personal suffering and determine the success of their outcomes by the number of people receiving rice each day as a food supplement (for example). Movement of goods and services and the number of heads being addressed each day are the focus.

#3B: Community Systems Focus (Development Organizations)

When development organizations prioritize changing systems by addressing the key challenges that are contributing to poverty, they do so to enhance these communities and to lead to better outcomes for all the people in the community. Typically, they will bring particular services or a group of services—such as education, clean water, food aid, and a medical clinic—to address some of the direst struggles in the community that are causing the most harm.

Outcomes

Over time, all three of these models require ongoing foreign funding in the thousands, millions, and billions of dollars globally. They have no realistic structure to build even a hope of locally sourced funding (a required path for sustainability). The only perceived potential funding source is that of the local governments, which are already overtaxed, in the hope they will take over the aid and subsidy programs for the longer term. This does not happen.

Therefore, all these types of organizations depend on individuals, organizations, and foreign governments to fund these dependency programs, departments, and individual workers in perpetuity, as they provide aid resources, salaries of aid workers, and so on. The funding comes because of the good work that they do in seeking to lift people from their dire state to a less dire state, hoping that this will create long-term change in people's lives in positive and dynamic ways. Unfortunately, they do not include opportunities for wealth creation, and therefore the poor cannot participate in their own economic emancipation.

These three approaches regularly cross over into each other's territories in a variety of ways and are not "pure" in the forms described above; rather these are simply the dominant models for how they respectively engage communities.

WHICH TYPE OF ORGANIZATIONS ARE MOST LIKELY TO BRING LONG-TERM CHANGE?

Development Organizations

Development organizations are closest in nature to what can succeed, as they access the total situation in poor communities from a more systemic approach. It is only through systemic changes that we see sustainable growth and development come about in efficacious ways. This also means that there can be effective partnerships between development organizations and more specialized aid groups. So, the one that funds clinics can fund a clinic, or the one that builds schools can partner and build the school. The specialized purveyors bring their expertise and a proven track record in that area.

Many of these require a high degree of specialized knowledge to put in place that particular missing piece. When all of them are properly coordinated to partner together and cover the particular missing pieces in that community, we are on a very good beginning path. The following are important and essential questions to ask as we engage communities in transformation:

1. What is working and what is not working?
2. What are those missing pieces?
3. Who are the best potential partners?
4. Who has expertise in the areas of the missing pieces?

In this way a team can be assembled with an appropriate level of expertise and resources. This also requires coordination between many and varied organizations with their unique cultures, so it is no small undertaking.

INTERRELATIONSHIPS

All three of these organization types provide important services and play particular roles; they also have limitations and weaknesses based on their structures, emphases, and roles. Most often they will not readily partner with another entity for a variety of reasons that we have already discussed, which can make this coordination task difficult. With different authority structures, rules, protocols, timelines, policies, and urgencies, coordination can be difficult to nearly impossible. Add in corruption at the local level and the busyness of talking to many potential partners while overall effectiveness grinds to a halt.

Building Connections

In one particular country, a local church partnered with a graduate student from the Full Gospel denomination and built a school, preschool, and seminary over time. While I was visiting there, another organization requested that I make introductions for their medical mission, which supplies high-tech medical equipment from the United States as well as nurses' training and organizational expertise to support hospitals and clinics. Over the next eighteen months—after much confusion, many phone calls, protocol challenges, and misstarts—the Presbyterian, Baptist, and Full Gospel denominations began working with the Medical

Benevolence Foundation out of Houston, Texas, and it was, in the end, a blessing for all.

Shared Fields

Many times, all three of these types of organizations and approaches find themselves in "competition" with each other on the ground and functioning at seemingly cross- or counter-purposes. That is not to mention the ongoing, accompanying challenges of corruption, greed, malice, bribery, and the like making their work that much more difficult.

Shared Funding Sources

All three also rely on funding from wealthy benefactors—whether governments, large charities, individuals, or other entities. Many times they are sharing the same potential pool of benefactors; therefore, they are in competition for the funds to assist the poor. They must set themselves apart, for fear they will lose a donor if that donor finds a different organization as a better fit for support.

Why do these efforts so often not succeed? It has to do with failure to analyze for *all* the missing pieces and problems that the community faces, as well as those latent problems and challenges that we have yet to discover. On the positive side, we regularly fail to identify the local resources present—in leadership, culture of service, and potential for mobilization—that are right in front of our eyes.

The Key Missing Ingredients

1. Local, creative, entrepreneurial, globally educated leaders.

2. Economic (capital) investment into medium-size and larger businesses for expanded employment and increased wages, leading to economic diversification and sustainability.

3. A sustainability plan led by an independent, local board with authority over the businesses whose profits fund the charitable ministries and enterprises established.

4. Effective involvement and cooperation of all community leaders, including religious leaders, as leaders of change.

COMBINING THE MISSING PIECES AND PROCESSES

As stated above, even the best of development organizations tend to focus on bringing a missing program into a community along with aid—all funded from outside the community. The addition of a critical program is beneficial, but there remain two challenges: first, the need of a strategy for systematic expansion of the local economy, and second, creating an income stream via long-term, local funding opportunities.

Absent ongoing, local funding resources, we are dooming the project to being dependent on outside funding to keep them going, which is unsustainable. Likewise, it does not help with the first deficit of economically stimulating the community into expanding and growing. By addressing these key missing ingredients for leadership and economic development, we can create long-term, sustainable, internal expansion that blesses the community as a whole and expands outwards to other communities, creating a fruitful, multiplier effect.

50

Key Role of Religious Leaders

OFTEN EXCLUDED

LOCAL RELIGIOUS LEADERS ARE often excluded from involvement in local development work, as the aid organizations deem themselves and their work to be non-religious. This is further compounded by the fealty to the funding sources that they utilize—from governments to foundations and other large funders. Particularly what is called "proselytizing" is singled out as a function not to be funded.

Proselytizing is excluded because it is viewed as distracting from the primary goal of bringing physical and practical solutions to peoples suffering. It is also viewed as factionalism, wherein one religious group will administer it in one way, and another will view it differently. This phenomenon places the aid organization in the position of determining which theology or belief system is the correct one. They have neither the expertise nor the interest to engage in determining these differences, and they consequently get caught in religious squabbles.

Therefore, religious teaching is easily conflated with proselytizing and viewed as superfluous to the primary work of delivering aid and community development. But this benign exclusion ignores the critical and essential leadership structures of the local community that are required for long-term success.

KEY ROLE

In the smaller villages, the religious leader is one of two or three main leaders, and often the most trusted leader carrying the greatest level of sway in the community for achieving goals and engaging in new cooperative ventures. Religious leaders are gatekeepers to the community.

The Challenges

Without their enthusiastic support, most projects will go nowhere. In the West, religious leaders are often ignored and considered largely irrelevant unless they venture into making public political statements, an action that is deemed "outside of their territory." They are not seen as being important in the community life overall. Rather, they are viewed as playing a respected role only in the sphere of their religious community (church, synagogue, mosque, or temple).

The other challenge present for utilizing the religious leaders in the community effectively is getting them to cooperate with each other. This requires identifying which of the religious leaders in the area has influence to gather the others—a task that can be particularly challenging, as having the support of one does not mean you have the support of them all. Likewise, each of them will have their own wishes and desires, and if they do not believe that they are being appropriately respected, they will either directly or tacitly withdraw their support, thereby undermining the overall work to be done.

Religious Leaders Working Together

One must tread carefully in these relationships. A whole book could be written on how to navigate these effectively, but space doesn't permit that here. The best strategy is to identify a key leader or influencer, defined in the Bible as the *person of peace* (see Luke 10:6). This person will be one of the key leaders listed above, with outside exposure and the ability to coordinate the other community leaders in a cooperative way. Many, if not most, will claim that they have that capacity, which only proves the desire to be influential. The real skill will only be proven as that key leader is able to perform the essential function of leading other leaders cooperatively in forward, unified action.

FAÇADE OF INCLUSION

When local religious leaders are included in the process by NGOs or aid organizations, it is usually only to coopt their influence to gather the people for the purposes of the outside organization. The religious leaders will be invited to "understand" what the aid organization is doing and to publicly support the work, but their leadership skills, ability, and knowledge will not be solicited or even considered to be an important asset in the community by the aid organization—let alone inform the community development work. Clearly, the aid organization has the resources, and they have their specified program, so they must be the experts by default. Take it or leave it.

Human Challenge: Arrogance and Resources

The possession of resources is regularly equated with greater personal knowledge and ability; however, this is a fallacy. As an example, imagine someone who has a billion dollars going to a nuclear power plant and telling the technicians how to run the reactor, solely because of that individual's wealth. A billion dollars doesn't make you more knowledgeable about nuclear physics than a nuclear engineer; it just means you have more money in your wallet or bank account. It is a subtle self-deception that happens to human beings when they have the authority over a particular resource merely to distribute it. They begin to ascribe to themselves the quality or value of that resource and deem themselves to have exclusive knowledge and expertise that goes well beyond a simple distribution function. This notion is completely false and excessively common.

COMING TOGETHER: NECESSARY LEADERSHIP ALIGNMENTS

Each of the local leaders has a role to play and particular strengths and weaknesses. However, when they can all work well together, it is the best of situations overall. Contrastingly, when any of them fail intentionally or otherwise, or there is a constant encroaching into each other's areas of influence and authority, there tend to be limitations and failures that result from this crossing of boundaries. Local leaders will have a view of their relative authority in relation to other leaders in the community and will want to maintain and display their potential and ability to promote their actual status as they perceive it. If one of these leaders feels slighted by another in any way, significant problems will ensue.

51

Putting It All Together

THE GOOD: INCLUDING ALL THE MISSING PIECES

IT IS THE MISSING pieces and practices that we have seen that ultimately help to fulfill our vision. We cannot overstate the value of raising up transformed, outside-educated, local leaders and utilizing capital resources for growth through medium-sized businesses. These local businesses, in turn, support their community through schools, clinics, and other essential initiatives. They will grow under healthy, local authority and accountability, being led by a diverse board that embraces the mission. The practices that we have repeated throughout this book, when prayerfully implemented, are the greatest harbingers of expansive opportunity and growth. They are proven effective and capitalize on the vast human resources that we want to positively affect in the first place.

THE BAD: WORKING AROUND CHALLENGING OBSTACLES TO GLORIOUS, FRUITFUL RETURNS

Our real competitors are corruption, pride, arrogance, and ignorance—by any or all parties in their unique ways. We must also jump the hurdles of incompetence and indifference by those internal and external to the project who believe that they must be shown proper patronage, payoffs, and deference before they will contribute to the new initiatives. Despite the many challenges that we have reviewed, the plans that God has given you to establish will continue to move forward in healthy, expeditious, and affirmative ways, by his grace and for his glory.

Watching God fruitfully multiply and expand resources in a community and region is miraculous to behold. Just like in the Parable of the Talents, it does not follow a formula of equity for all, but instead it opens an expansive and diverse landscape of accessible opportunity using the different gifts that God has placed in each person in the community.

SEEING LIVES AND COMMUNITIES TRANSFORMED

Indeed, there is a better way, and we now have eyes to see, identify, and sidestep the same practices that have myopically focused on transfer payments and long-term, programmatic subsidies with limited and failed outcomes. Our mission of transformation—lifting people to encounter the God who made them and loves them and wants to see their fullest potential realized—has everything to do with how people will take best advantage of the opportunities presented to them. It is God who called us all to be people who change the world and reproduce that in others to bring God's kingdom on earth as it is in heaven (see Matthew 6:9–13).

In a future volume, we intend to cover the manifold *Project Implementation Steps* that will help likeminded leaders bring new initiatives to life. This emerging adventure includes essential ingredients like prayer, the statement of your vision, prioritization of agenda items, identification of resources, formation of boards, pilot projects, and much, much more. Moving forward in hope and humility, we will together embrace the extraordinary opportunities to create a vast, panoramic landscape of blessing wherever God calls us. *Soli Deo gloria.*

Conclusion

WE WERE MADE TO change the world! Our brothers and sisters around the world are not looking for a handout—they are looking for a hand up. We could spend our lives in search of new things and experiences, fancy titles, and influence. But these are the great deceptions. They take a long time to achieve, and once achieved, they provide little or no reward like we anticipated.

Rather we were made for great things. All of God's people are made for great things, but there is this little secret: *The great things in life are accomplished through connections*, through working together to imagine and create things bigger than our own ability or imagination. "But as it is written: Eye has not seen, nor ear heard, nor have entered into the heart of man the things which God has prepared for those who love Him" (1 Corinthians 2:9, NKJV).

God made you special, and you do not need to wait until you have made your fortune to make a difference in the world. People are lost in poverty, addiction, and lack of food—all tied to a lack of opportunity and tangible resources to produce wealth. We all need someone to believe in us, to tell us, "You can do this. I believe in you! God believes in you!" What are you waiting for? Get on your knees and pray and get going. The reward is tremendous and eternal.

You can do this. God has called us to change the world, and we no longer need to relocate ourselves across the globe to make an enduring difference in the lives of people in a sustainable, flourishing, and multiplying way. People whom you were created to partner with are praying right now—in desperation that someone would hear their plea and partner with them—to share in the local knowledge that they possess but also to add the specific expertise or capital that they lack.

You are the experts in your fields of work and study. These talents and abilities were given to you for the joy of sharing them to the benefit and growth of a whole community by supporting a local team of key leaders. These abilities are invaluable. You are more than a donation; you are more than just a financial contribution. You are a talented, committed, and compassionate person with specific gifts and abilities, built for relationships that have lasting effect and reflect the love of the one who created you.

As you prayerfully gather together your team, remember your calling. Think of the children who will receive education and opportunity. Consider the adults whose literacy will free them to start their own businesses and provide for their families a home, education, and medical care that they have longed to provide. Imagine the churches that will be planted, the miracles that will be performed.

The reward is endless as one life touches the next, as people engage with their church and bless their community. As they continue to grow and expand, they will affect other communities around them. This is what we were made for. These are the things that can never be taken away and that endure into eternity.

Be blessed.
Be fruitful.
Be generous with you.
Be grand in your humility as you learn.
Pray fervently, as attacks will come.
Embrace the miracles as you pray.
Share what God has done and what you have learned.
Be generous together for the glory of God.

Peace.

Bibliography

Adams, John. "Letter from John Adams to Massachusetts Militia, 11 October 1798." https://founders.archives.gov/documents/Adams/99–92-02–3102.

Badriaki, Michael Bamwesigye. *When Helping Works: Alleviating Fear and Pain in Global Missions*. Eugene, OR: Wipf & Stock, 2017.

Benner, Jeff A. *The Ancient Hebrew Lexicon of the Bible*. College Station, TX: Virtualbookworm, 2005.

Benyus, Janine. *Biomimicry: Innovation Inspired by Nature*. New York: William Morrow, 1997.

Corbett, Steve, and Brian Fikkert. *When Helping Hurts: How to Alleviate Poverty Without Hurting the Poor. . . and Yourself*. Chicago: Moody, 2009.

Courtois, Stéphane, et al. *The Black Book of Communism*. Cambridge, MA: Harvard University Press, 1999.

Crouch, Chad. "Lesslie Newbigin." https://www.youtube.com/watch?v=b5BO4oCUYXs.

Kennedy, John F. "President John F. Kennedy's Inaugural Address (1961)." https://www.archives.gov/milestone-documents/president-john-f-kennedys-inaugural-address.

"Lexicon: Strong's H5493—*sûr*." https://www.blueletterbible.org/lexicon/h5493/kjv/wlc/0–1.

"PEACE Plan Model." https://www.thepeaceplan.com/thepeaceplanmodel.

Poverty, Inc. Acton Institute, 2014.

Savory, Allan. "How to fight desertification and reverse climate change." https://www.ted.com/talks/allan_savory_how_to_fight_desertification_and_reverse_climate_change?language=en.

Savory, Allan, et al. *Holistic Management Handbook*. Washington, DC: Island, 2019.

www.ingramcontent.com/pod-product-compliance
Lightning Source LLC
Chambersburg PA
CBHW070607270326
41926CB00013B/2455